# Moccasin Trails

## Meredith & Linda Anderson

The Cover:
Photo by
Cover and interior Pictures used with permission.
Drawing: Brooke Abbey
Other Interior photos: Property of the author under his copyright ©
Map: Enchanted Learning.com

# Moccasin Trails

Manufactured in the United States of America

**To:** The adventure Lover in all of us...
Especially to people who like to read out loud... and
to
Everyone that listens.

# Acknowledgments:

I would like to offer special thanks to those who encouraged me in this endeavor, especially Nikki Hansen, retired Professor and Head of the English Department from Weber State University in Ogden, Utah, my alma mater.

I would be remiss not to mention my wife, Linda, a historian and author in her own right, who became my best friend over fifty-two years ago when I was a young sailor in Uncle Sam's Seventh Fleet. Ted Horsman, Dr. James Tinnell and Marie Hollenbeck.

# M.I.A.

# History is recorded by the victorious.

If it weren't for the white man and his penchant for writing and making a record of everything, the Indian would have no history at all.

Yes, it is argued that the Indian made pictographs on skins and passed down verbal history, but this is generally for one tribe, one clan, one incident.

The big picture, the good and the bad was best chronicled by the white man and the power of his press.

When the Indian learned to read and write, either in his own language, like the Cherokee or in the white man's tongue, then and only then did he become his own historian.

# America's First Mountain Man

In 1803 the United States government bought what would be known as the "Louisiana Purchase" from Napoleon of France at a cost of about a penny an acre - 15 million dollars. This purchase doubled the size of the United States.

The government had taken on a "laissez-faire" attitude. A disposition that the government would not be involved in anyone's business. This created an economic environment in which transactions between private parties are free from government restrictions, tariffs, and subsidies, with only enough regulations to protect property rights.

President Thomas Jefferson commissioned an expedition known then as the Corps of Discovery.

1

In 1803 The Corps of Discovery was to explore and map the newly acquired territory, to find a practical route across the western half of the continent, and to establish an American presence in this territory before Britain, Spain or any other European powers tried to claim it. The campaign's secondary objectives were scientific and economic: to study the area's plants, animal life, and geography, and to establish trade with local American Indian tribes.

One of Thomas Jefferson's goals was to find the most direct and practicable water route across the country for the purposes of commerce. He also placed special importance on declaring US sovereignty over the land occupied by the many different Indian tribes along the Missouri River, and getting an accurate sense of the resources in the recently purchased territory.

LEWIS AND CLARK
EXPEDITION
1804-1806

John Colter's father emigrated to Virginia from Ireland in 1700. John was born in Virginia in 1774 and shortly there after his family moved to Kentucky where he spent his youth trailing through the backwoods hunting, trapping and exploring.

At the age of twenty-nine John was a strapping lad of 5 feet 10 inches in height and weighed 150 pounds.

Colter met Meriwether Lewis in Pittsburgh, Pennsylvania where Lewis was waiting on the construction of a keel boat.

Lewis was impressed by the outdoor knowledge and skills that Colter displayed and on October 15, 1803 he enlisted him into the Corps of Discovery as a Private at the pay of five dollars a month.

The Corps of Discovery soon became know as the Lewis and Clark Expedition.

Before starting the expedition, both Lewis and Clark were away from camp, leaving Sergeant Ordway in charge. Several members of the company, Colter among them, disobeyed orders issued by the sergeant.

When Meriwether Lewis returned to camp, all of the disobedient members were restricted to camp for ten days. Colter became angry and said he would like to shoot Ordway. For this, Colter was court-martialed.

When the court-martial was reviewed, Colter was allowed to give an apology and his promise that this behavior would not continue. He was reinstated.

During the expedition, it was quickly discovered that Colter was one of the best hunters in the company. As a result, he was often sent out alone ahead of the company to scout the surrounding countryside for table meat.

He was often trusted with responsibilities that went beyond hunting and being a woodsman. He played a key role in helping the expedition find passes through the Rocky Mountains.

In one instance, Colter was handpicked by Clark to deliver a message to Lewis, who had been held up at a Shoshone camp. The message indicated that it would be unwise to follow a planned route along the Salmon River.

In another instance he was charged with retracing a route in the Bitterroot Mountains to recover lost horses and supplies, and not only did he return with some of the supplies and horses, but he also brought deer to give to the hospitable Nez Perce tribes. This fresh meat would also strengthen members of the company that had become ill.

Colter never reported for sick-call and with good strong health he and only a few others were allowed to leave camp during stops for illness recuperation.

Another major contribution Colter made to the Lewis and Clark Expedition was leading the expedition down the Bitterroot Mountains, allowing access to the Snake River, Columbia River and subsequently, the Pacific Ocean.

On one occasion, while hunting far ahead of the

main party, Colter encountered three Tushepawe Flatheads. Through non-verbal peace symbols and communication, Colter was able to persuade the Flatheads to abandon their search for two Shoshones who had stolen twenty three head of horses, and accompany him to the expedition's camp.

One of the young Flatheads agreed to act as the party's guide down the mountains and through Flathead country, a great advantage in challenging and unfamiliar terrain plagued by a scarcity of game.

Once at the mouth of the Columbia River, Colter was among a small group selected to explore to the shores of the Pacific Ocean. This group also explored the seacoast north of the Columbia into present-day Washington state.

After traveling thousands of miles, in 1806 the expedition returned to the Mandan villages in present-day North Dakota. There, they encountered Forest Hancock and Joseph Dickson, two frontiersmen of Colter's acquaintance, who were headed into the upper Missouri River country in search of furs.

On August 13, 1806, Lewis and Clark honorably discharged Colter, almost two months early, so that he could lead the two trappers back to the region they had explored.

Colter, Hancock, and Dixon ventured into the wilderness with 20 beaver traps, a two-year supply of ammunition, and numerous other small tools gifted to them by the expedition such as knives, rope, hatchets, and personal utensils.

After reaching a point where the Gallatin, Jefferson and Madison Rivers meet, known today as Three Forks, Montana, the trio managed to maintain their partnership for only two months.

After a falling out with Dixon, Colter and Hancock spent the winter of 1806-1807 at Three Forks.

Colter grew restless with taking shelter and ascended the canyon into the Sunlight Basin of modern-day Wyoming. This made him the first white man known to have ever entered this region.

He started back toward civilization in 1807, and was near the mouth of the Platte River, when he encountered Manuel Lisa, a founder of the Missouri Fur Trading Company, who was leading a party that included George Drouillard, John Potts, and Peter Weiser, all former members of the Lewis and Clark Expedition, towards the Rocky Mountains.

Colter, once again, decided to return to the wilderness, even though he would be in St. Louis in less than a week.

At the confluence of the Yellowstone and Bighorn Rivers, Colter helped build Fort Raymond. Afterwards he was sent by Manuel Lisa to search out the Crow Indian tribe and find out about the opportunities of establishing trade with them.

Colter left Fort Raymond in October of 1807 with his rifle and ammunition and a pack weighing roughly thirty five pounds. He traveled over five hundred miles to establish trade with the Crow nation.

During the winter, he explored the region that

we know as Yellowstone and Grand Teton National Parks. Colter reportedly visited at least one geyser basin, though it is now believed that he most likely was near present-day Cody, Wyoming, which at that time may have had some geothermal activity.

He then explored Jackson Hole at the foot of the Teton Range, later crossing Teton Pass into Pierre's Hole, known today as the Teton Basin in the state of Idaho.

After turning north and then east, he is believed to have encountered Yellowstone Lake, another location in which he may have seen geysers and other geothermal features.

He then went back to Fort Raymond, arriving in March or April 1808. Not only had Colter traveled hundreds of miles, unguided, he did so in the dead of winter, in a region in which nighttime temperatures in January are routinely $-30$ °F.

Colter got back to Fort Raymond and few believed his reports of geysers, bubbling mud pots and steaming pools of water. His reports of these features were ridiculed at first, and the region was somewhat jokingly referred to as "Colter's Hell."

It is believed that Colter's Hell referred to the region of 'Stinking Water,' now known as the Shoshone River, particularly the section running through Cody.

The river's original name was due to the presence of sulfur in the surrounding area. His detailed exploration of this region is the first by a white man of what later became the state of Wyoming.

In 1808, Colter and Potts, a former member of the Lewis and Clark Expedition, set out from Fort Raymond in the region near Three Forks, Montana. This mission was once more to negotiate trade agreements with local nations.

While leading a group of eight hundred Flathead and Crow Indians back to the trading fort, Colter's party was attacked by a band of Blackfeet numbering over fifteen-hundred. The Flatheads and Crows managed to force the Blackfeet into retreat, but Colter suffered a leg wound from an arrow.

This wound was not serious and Colter quickly recuperated and left Fort Raymond with Potts once more the following year.

The Blackfeet were trading partners with the French and Dutch that came out of Canada. They had guns and were well supplied. They had a great hatred for all Americans, this a leftover from the French and Indian War, the flames of which were constantly fanned by the French and Dutch traders.

In 1809, John Potts and John Colter were taking two canoes up the Jefferson River. Potts and Colter came upon a band of several hundred Blackfeet who demanded they come ashore. Colter guided his canoe ashore and was disarmed and stripped naked.

When Potts refused to bring his canoe ashore he was shot and wounded. He returned fire and killed one of the Indian warriors. He died immediately, riddled by a hail of bullets fired by the Indians on the shore. His body was brought ashore and hacked to pieces in front of Colter. Colter tried to protest, but was slapped across the face with a rifle butt.

The Blackfeet held a council and it was decided that he would be a little sport for several of the young warriors.

Colter was brought before the War Chief and told in the Crow language that he would be permitted to leave. A few seconds later a brave would be sent out after him for the purpose of killing him. A few seconds later another warrior would be sent and so on.

He stood in front of the Chief naked, knowing that he would be running for his life.

In keeping with the idea of 'good sportsmanship," the braves were not allowed to carry any 'long range weapons' such as guns or bows and arrows.

Colter had always been a  fast runner, but now, after several miles in his naked condition, he was exhausted and bleeding profusely from his nose which had been bashed by a rifle butt. He was far ahead of most of the Blackfeet, with only one that seemed to be closing on him.

He hid behind a large tree and as the warrior passed he leaped upon him with a choke hold from behind and managed to overcome the warrior.

As he stood he turned slightly and saw another brave not twenty yards behind and closing fast. He knew he had to act fast, but his legs were like jelly and he could feel them wobbling.

He took two steps toward the Indian and spread his arms screaming, "Come and get me!"

The warrior was surprised by the suddenness of this action, and perhaps stunned at the bloody appearance of Colter. He was now very close and as he attempted to stop, he was exhausted from running. He tried to raise his war lance for the attack, but he fell forward sticking his spear in the ground. The weight of his body was against the lance and it broke. Colter snatched up the pointed end, and pinned the brave to the earth.

Colter snatched up a blanket from the Indian he had killed and continued his run with several Indians following close behind.

He reached the Madison River, five miles from where he started. A large beaver dam was stretched across the Madison and he began to walk on it to cross to the other side. It was at this point that he was struck by genius. All of his backwoods experience was about to pay off. He dove into the clear water next to the beaver dam. When he saw the underwater entrance to the beaver lodge, he came up. The entrance hole was only large enough for his head but he could breath, no problem.

Soon the Blackfeet were crossing the dam trying to pick up his trail. He stayed in his lair and listened to the voices of disappointed braves as they wandered back and forth trying to pick up his trail.

Being unable to pick up his trail, the Blackfeet turned back toward their camp and left.

When it got dark, he climbed out of the beaver pond and walked eleven days to a trader's fort on the Little Big Horn.

In 1810, he was back at Fort Raymond and assisted with the construction of another fort located at Three Forks, Montana.

After returning from a fur pelt gathering trip, he discovered that two of his friends had been killed by the Blackfeet. This event convinced Colter to leave the wilderness for good and he returned to St. Louis before the end of 1810. He had been away from civilization for almost six years.

When he returned he contacted his "Corps of Discovery" commander, William Clark, and together they produced what became known as "A Map of Lewis and Clark's Track Across the Western Portion of North America from the Mississippi to the Pacific Ocean," which was published in 1814.

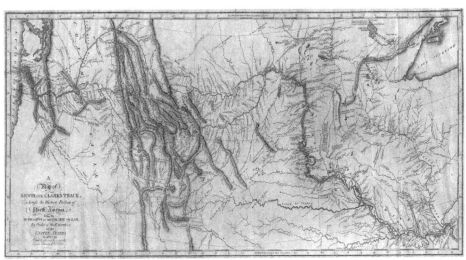

Upon his discharge, Colter had earned payment for 35 months and 26 days, totaling $179.33 dollars. However, a discrepancy in the books provided Colter with payment for the two months he had skipped to accompany Hancock and Dickson trapping. However, this over-payment may have been justified by Colter's significant work ethic and personal praise by Thomas Jefferson himself. In 1807, Colter's settlement was retracted after Congress passed a mandate supplying all members of the Corps of Discovery with doubled wages and land grants of 320 acres. Lewis personally took responsibility for Colter's reparations, and following Lewis' death and Colter's subsequent return to St. Louis, a court decided Colter was owed an amount of $377.60.

In St. Louis, Colter married a woman named Sallie and purchased a farm near Miller's Landing, Missouri, now New Haven, Missouri.

# The American Indian

In 1492 when Columbus came ashore in the West Indies, he thought he had circumnavigated the globe and he was arriving in India. As a result he called the indigenous people of the islands Indians.

Since that time, with over six hundred different tribes within the borders of the continental United States, these people are still called Indians.

The Indians did not have books or a written language. The elders of the tribe, usually the grandparents, were the ones who spent time with the children, teaching them laws, religion and history during work and counseling sessions. Children under twelve years of age spent at least two hours each day at the knee of an elder or grandparent learning.

Being taught by the elders, the first thing that was learned was respect for age and compassion for the younger. The "Great Spirit" was the guide in all situations. He was the creator of all things and gave and took life as he willed.

The only language that they had was their verbal tongue, so in many cases, one tribe could not speak to another tribe unless some member had gone to the trouble of learning their language and then they could be the interpreter.

The sun was a primary symbol in the strata of Indian religious belief and out of respect, he always set up his dwelling with the doorway facing eastward so he could always be greeted by the rising sun in the morning.

For the Sioux, it was believed that the "Great Spirit" made his home in the Black Hills of the Dakota mountains, much as the ancient Greeks believed that their gods lived atop Mount Olympus.

The Thunder Bird was believed to live atop the cloud-shrouded and snow-crested peaks causing rain, snow and storms that were gentle as well as those that were violent.

When a child was born, he or she was named by the grandmother and the medicine man. If the grandmother was deceased, the name was given by the oldest female living relative. The name was changed at the age of four to his permanent name, again by the grandmother. At that time the child was named after something that the "Great Spirit" had created or a name from the clan of his or her fraternal grandfather.

Indians did not know anything about "property rights," but they knew what was their "territory." When the white man came, they at first welcomed him as a friend, but it was not long before the Europeans began to flood into their territory.

At first they fought back but in a short time they were overwhelmed by the numbers and technology of the whites. They soon found it easier to make a deal, a treaty with the Europeans or move westward encroaching on other Indian territories.

Often, the other tribes were easier to defeat than the whites so they moved westward or to the north into Canada.

There were many disagreements between Indian and European cultures clashing over land, hunting rights, treaties made and broken by both sides and the overhanging threat of annihilation.

Due to the shear numbers of people and the advanced technologies of the growing United States, the Indians fought a war they could not win.

In defeat, they were relegated to lands no one else wanted. These lands were called reservations and they were guarded by the US Army to ensure that the Indians did not try to change their address.

# New England Wars

Five hundred years of silence had passed into oblivion for the natives that populated the area of New England. Having repelled the Norseman Thorvald from Greenland who attempted settlement of the area in the year 1000, the local band of Skroellings eventually were themselves replaced by an even more fierce race.

It was fortunate for the Pilgrims that they landed on Plymouth Bay on Christmas Day, 1620 and settled on land that had been wiped clean of population in recent years by a plague. The Pilgrims never made any attempts to convert outsiders to their faith, including the Natives they encountered in America and the nonbelievers who'd joined them as laborers in England. So encounters with the natives were looked at as something to be taken as part of their normal relations with others.

The Puritans of the Massachusetts Bay Colony which would later become Boston had a totally different philosophy. They were strict adherents to their religious beliefs, imposing imprisonment and punishment on those not in agreement. These differences between the Pilgrims and the Puritans would later determine how they treated the Indians.

Three months without contact with the natives was interrupted in mid-March of 1621 when the Pilgrims were startled to see a tall Indian with straight black hair and wearing only a leather band of fringe around his waist, walking boldly down their streets.

To their further surprise he greeted them in English which he had learned from the sailing ship crews that frequented the fishing areas. His name was Samoset, a chief, from a northern area. He informed them that the local tribe of Indians numbering about sixty warriors was led by Chief Massasoit.

He had been dispatched by Massasoit to investigate the strangers. He soon brought into the colony the legendary Squanto who had been taken captive and sold into slavery by an unethical sea captain. Squanto had learned European culture while living in England after Spanish monks had paid for his freedom. From that day until his death from disease a few years later he was ever attached to the Pilgrims and their cause.

Massasoit pledged himself to a treaty of peace which he kept throughout his lifetime. The treaty promised that he and the colonists would assist each other against their mutual enemies and recompense each party for any injuries done by individuals on either side. The peace that came allowed the colonists to learn how to plant corn and fertilize it with fish from the streams.

With this close association came the nuisance of the Indians being too friendly. Soon they realized it was easier to beg food from the white man than to hunt for it. This led to a group of Indians who themselves verged on starvation after having saved the white men.

This friendliness with the white men brought hostility down upon Massasoit's head. The fierce Narragansett, a warlike tribe living to the south, were hostile toward any intruders and vowed to eradicate them. The Pilgrims received an unexpected arrival of 35 young men in late autumn 1621, a welcome augmentation of the 19 men still able to bear arms out of 55 male colonists who had survived the winter. Unfortunately, brought no provisions or clothing and became a burden.

This was a sign to the hostile tribes that the colony would weaken on its own. A Narragansett declaration of war (a snake skin filled with arrows) came by messenger to the Plymouth colony. Filling the skin with powder and balls, Governor Bradford returned it. This bold action staved off the Narragansett for the winter.

In July 1622 another large party of two ships for a new settlement arrived from England. The Pilgrims were dismayed by these strangers who were idle, worthless and ate the green corn before it matured. They found their own site but by midwinter both colonies were starving because of the foolish consumption of green corn by the new arrivals and their failure to plant their own crop. This forced both colonies to survive by trading with the Indians.

The newcomers enraged even the Massachusetts and soon war was at hand.

The new colony deserved the extinction that was proposed for them. They would not dig for clams to stave off famine as the Pilgrims did, but proposed to attack the Massachusetts Indians and steal their corn. But the Indians had no corn to give. The Indians' wrath was incited to eradicate these begging, sniveling interlopers, but they knew they could not spare Plymouth either for the revenge that would surely follow.

Captain Miles Standish warned the laggards to set up a defense and, taking eight armed men, pursued the two Indian ringleaders. He knew they would not meet him and his men in a fair fight so he planned to surprise them in some manner. Two of the villains, named Pecksuot and Wittuwamet, had bragged before Standish of their plans to kill him. On this meeting they taunted him for his small size and bragged of the excellence of their knives.

Standish was calm, taking his time, and the next day he found himself alone with three other Englishmen in the same room as the ring leaders and two other Indians.

He ordered the door barred. Pecksuot drew his finely sharpened knife and hand-to-hand combat commenced among the two warring parties, four against four. Standish slew his opponent while the other three Englishmen killed the other ring leader and one of his followers. The fourth was captured for future hanging at Plymouth colony before the assembled people. Thus peace was assured for the

Plymouth colony that lasted for twelve years.

✳✳✳

By 1633 there were seven strong towns and a coastal area dotted with settlements along the Connecticut River. It was on the Connecticut that the trouble began which only the valor and good fortune of the colonists saved them from extinction. To the east and north lay the Pequots, the most fearsome of the New England tribes. They had watched as Springfield and Hartford and a couple other towns had been erected. Disputes over property, hunting, selling of alcohol to the Indians and dishonest traders stirred the pot.

The new Pequot chief, Sassacus, was a terror to the Mohegans, the Narragansets and their neighbors. To control the wampum trade, they had subjugated other tribes in the area and on the offshore islands. They had established a tributary confederacy of dozens of tribes that paid homage to the Pequot through force, diplomacy and marriage.

The Pequot and the Dutch had controlled the trade and the tribes subjugated to the Pequot saw the incursion of the English traders into the area as an opportunity to break free of fierce Dutch masters.

The Englishmen felt superior to their savage neighbors and made no effort to understand their plight, caught between two factions, Pro-English and Pro-Dutch as the Dutch had expanded their trading area. This fractionalization of the Pequot culminated in Sassacus (pro-Dutch) taking control and his main opponent for chief, Uncas, (pro-English) who was his son-in-law, taking his people and leaving to establish a separate tribe called the Mohegans. In addition, 1633-34 brought a smallpox epidemic to the tribe which, along with Uncas' desertion, had robbed the tribe of half its population.

When trader captains commenced to push their crafts up the Connecticut River, the time had come for the Englishmen of the Massachusetts Bay Colony to face these fierce warriors.

In the summer of 1634 John Stone, an English smuggler and privateer, soon brought the tensions to a head with his unabashed abuse of the Indians. He had abducted two Western Niantic (clients of the Pequot) men and forced them to guide him to the Connecticut River. He and his whole crew were slain by the Niantic as they slept.

The Indians, fearful of the reprisal of the colonists, sent gifts to the colony and claimed the men had been slain by their own company who set off a powder blast after they had killed the captain for inflicting injury to one of their sachem, Tatobem. Tatobem had actually been taken prisoner and slain by Dutch traders. They argued so loudly of their promised good behavior that it was allowed to pass as some in Boston felt it was good riddance to have Stone done in.

On June 26, 1636 Captain John Oldham (founder of Wethersfield, Connecticut) and his crew was found slain, his trading boat, having been overrun by a sizable party of fourteen Block Island Indians who were found on board and subsequently driven either overboard or captured by a passing vessel.

Having been driven off course from Connecticut to Long Island by weather, Captain John Gallup, with only two men and two boys aboard, but all heavily armed and ready for combat, forced the savages to abandon ship by ramming her repeatedly. They came aboard with only four Indians left.

Two savages came up from the hatches and surrendered. One was tied and bound; another Gallup tied and threw into the sea. He found Oldham's body under an old sail, his body stripped naked and missing all its limbs. With the two remaining red men below, he fastened down the hatches and set sail.

When news reached Massachusetts Bay, a force of seventy men commanded by Captain Endicott went forth to punish the murderers.

To combat the Indians who tended to spread out into small fighting forces, several commanders were assigned to smaller configurations of fighting men.

Having laid anchor and seen a lone Indian walking the shoreline in a most aggrieved manner, Captain Underhill made for the shore in a boat accompanied by a dozen armed men. They were met by a barrage of fifty or sixty archers hidden behind the brush. On seeing the soldiers fight through the harsh surf and wade ashore, the Rock Island Indians turned on their heels when the bullets started to fly.

Gov. Endicott landing on Block Island.

The next day the colonists spent burning and spoiling all settlements and provisions on the island. They killed and wounded some fourteen Indians in the expedition and laid waste to much corn, Indian wigwams and beautiful mats and baskets full of provisions.

Returning to the nearest trading fort, Fort Saybrook, Endicott was lambasted by the commander, Lion Gardner, who had opposed the raid. He knew the soldiers had raised the wrath of the Indians and his settlement would soon feel the results, since his corn fields which provided for their provisions were two miles away. He lamented that they had done just enough to enrage the Indians and not enough to teach them to fear the colonists.

Captain Endicott sailed away without leaving reinforcements. Abandoning Gardner to bear the brunt of the Indian's revenge. From here they sailed north and burned a few Pequot wigwams then went home to Boston.

In a short time, in the isolated clearings along the Connecticut River, whole families fell to the toma- hawk, their crops and homes consumed in flame and dark smoke that sent a terrible message sky- ward.

Fort Saybrook held off the attackers through the wise leadership of Lieutenant Gardner who immedi- ately dispatched his men to gather in the corn.

He left five men in the strong house to guard the corn while he took the loaded boat back to the fort. Three of them disregarded his orders and went tur- key hunting. The Pequots shot all three, one escap- ing - the other two they tortured to death. When Gardner's boat returned, they found only two men whom they rescued, abandoning the rest of the corn. As they sailed away, they turned to see the strong house afire.

One of the settlers, a Mr. Mitchell, prevailed on the commander to let him take his own men to harvest his hay. Gardner tried to talk him out of it, even giving him instructions on how to leave a guard at the boat and scour the field with dogs under guard before trying to retrieve the crop. This advice was disregarded and when they commenced to harvest without first securing the perimeter, the Pequot killed three of the men. Mr. Mitchell's brother, the minister of Cambridge, they roasted alive.

The Indians sent the boat down river in the spring with one body aboard, the other body with an arrow stuck in its skull having been thrown in the river and recovered by the men at the fort.

The next months were spent in trying to outwit the Pequot who would creep upon the fort during the night or hide in the forest to spring on any work party that was sent out. In his own shrewd manner, Gardner used concealed traps such as doors with sharpened nails around the perimeter hid in the undergrowth.

In February 1637 a gang of ten men and three dogs were sent out to clear the weeds around the fort's walls which facilitated the secretive advances of their enemy. When a party of attackers sprang upon them, two Englishmen threw down their guns and ran for their lives. Two more in the reeds were shot and killed immediately, leaving Gardner and five other men to fight their way home. Two more were shot dead in the retreat, the survivors all fighting with swords despite numerous gun shot wounds.

Only the intercession of some of the settlers prevented Gardner from hanging the cowards.

The Connecticut settlers were now surrounded by five thousand warriors. The Pequot set up a parlay with their old enemies, the Narragansets, trying to convince them to join in the fight. Roger Williams in the dead of winter went to the Narraganset council fires and out-talked the Pequots in their efforts.

Williams, a dissenter who supported religious freedom, had been exiled from Massachusetts Bay and had purchased land from the Narragansett to establish Providence, Rhode Island. He became the go-between with the Narragansett who sided with the English, and, as a result, became the most powerful tribe in southern New England.

Finding little gain to continue to attack Fort Saybrook, on April 23, 1637 the Indians turned toward Wethersfield, killing nine and capturing two young girls who were later ransomed by Dutch traders.

In May, 1637 Massachusetts and Plymouth responded to the calls for help, sending two hundred men and six hundred pounds sterling. But before

these reinforcements could arrive, ninety volunteers under Captain John Mason mustered at Hartford. They were joined by seventy Mohegans under
their chief, Uncas. They met Captain Underhill with
twenty men at Fort Saybrook.

Uneasy with the Mohegans, the settlers felt Uncas had to demonstrate an act of war that would
prevent future reconciliation with their old enemies,
the Pequot. Uncas wanted to plunge into the fray
that very day, but it being Sunday, waited until the
next, bringing back six Pequot heads and one prisoner. The unfortunate prisoner was put to the torture by the Mohegans, one leg tied to a tree and
the other tied to twenty men who tore him to pieces
until Underhill mercifully shot him in the head. Thus
convinced of Uncas' loyalty, Underhill took his men
up river to meet Mason coming down river in his
great slow ship.

The force had been told to land at the Pequot River and move inland. Mason knew this was what the
Pequot's expected and would be waiting for him.
His plan to sail up the river and land, instead, deep
in Narragansett land was refused until divine intervention was sought by the minister on board the
ship in order to get the others to disregard written
orders. God's will prevailed.

Now reinforced with a great number of Narragansett, their Indian allies numbered five hundred.

Each Narragansett had come solemnly into the
circle of fire and vowed to slay many men in their

gallantry. After a twelve mile march in the heat that sent many a man down, the Narragansett cringed in the rear of the column, some even slipping away back to their homes.

The force encircled the nearest stockaded village of the Pequots near what is now New Haven, Connecticut. Resting their heads on rocks and listening to the riotous cries and proclamations coming from the festivities inside, every Englishman and Indian ally knew tomorrow's fight would determine the fate of the colony. Those who listened heard the boasting of a war party that would start tomorrow for the Connecticut with much slaughter of settlers to follow.

The next morning the white men covered the two miles to the fort and called for their Indian allies to come forward for the attack. None were to be found. At last Uncas appeared with Wequash, a former Pequot native as their guide. He reported to Mason that the Indians were behind and exceedingly afraid. Mason told them to watch how Englishmen fought and then come forward. Their Indian allies trembled at the bravery of the white men who drew near for the attack.

The stockade had two entrances and inside two lanes of seventy wigwams. Most of the inhabitants were old men, women and children, Sassacus having taken most of his braves off on a raiding party. No sentinel gave the alarm for none was posted. A dog bark woke the first Pequot who shouted,

Owanux!

The soldiers let loose a volley that had a terrible effect on the surprised Pequots. As the soldiers moved into the compound, the fighting was hand-to-hand. Within minutes they had lost two dead and twenty wounded, 50% of their fighting force inside the compound.

Unable to save the wigwams for plunder as the Indians rallied behind them, Mason ordered them fired - soon the whole stockade was ablaze and the Englishmen surrounded the compound. No mercy was shown to those who tried to escape. Beautiful young maidens and young children fell as did the blood-thirsty and cruel warriors to the rifle or to the tomahawk of the Mohegans and Narragansett had suddenly appeared at the sight of the Englishmen fighting for their lives. Only fifteen Pequots survived of the six or seven hundred caught inside.

This party was still in grave danger, far from the ships and mustering only fifty-five men. The Pequots could still rouse five hundred warriors from their second stockaded village.

Taking up their wounded, the men from Connecticut began the march to the Pequot River where they had directed their ships to rendezvous.

They were soon attacked by three hundred Indians from the second stockade. On discovering the burned village, they had stomped, yelled and tore their hair, chasing the Englishmen in a violent rage. A volley slowed them down.

The Narragansett and Mohegans were horrified by the English way of fighting; to them it was too furious and killed too many men.

The Narragansett now deserted in terror and were soon cut off and surrounded. Captain Underhill, with a detachment, went to their aid in time to save them.

The Indian allies now carried the wounded so all the soldiers could fight. The Englishmen pushed forward firing into every bush and keeping a constant look out. Finally, the flags of the ships were sighted and the Pequots fell back at this.

Captain Mason, a pious Puritan who had narrowly escaped death, exclaimed that "God was over them and that He laughed at his enemies to scorn, making them as a fiery oven. Thus did the Lord judge among the heathen, filling the place with dead bodies."

And the equally if not more pious Dr. Mather afterward wrote: "It was supposed that no less than 500 or 600 Pequod souls were brought down to hell that day. Happily a better Christian spirit now prevails."

This may seem a heartless condemnation to our modern ears, but to these men who sought God's instruction in all matters of their lives, the battle had been won because the Lord had deemed it so. And with the odds in battle so stacked against the Englishmen, it must have seemed a miracle to them to have not only survived but awarded the victory.

On board the ships were the Plymouth reinforcements led by Captain Patrick. The wounded and all the original volunteers were put on board and sent back to Fort Saybrook. Patrick and the Indian allies marched overland to the fort. One body of Pequot was encountered which fell back and they did not pursue, having had their fill of fighting for the day.

When they reached the fort, Gardner greeted them with a great many guns. All the volunteers were released to return to their homes with a heroes welcome.

As for the Pequots, they condemned Chief Sassacus and fled to New York killing all English they met on the way. Hundreds fell into the hands of the Mohegans and the Narragansett. Shortly the one hundred and twenty men from Massachusetts Bay arrived and the decision was made to go with Captain Mason and his forty men and pursue the fleeing Pequots. Sailing along the shores, they were able to easily capture several bands of fugitives who were weak from hunger and encumbered by their families.

A large group was found hiding in a swamp near Newport. Thomas Stanton, the interpreter from Fort Saybrook, insisted on going into the swamp. He came out leading two hundred old men, women and children. The warriors would not surrender. Sixty or seventy broke through the guard and escaped only to be cut down by the tribes they sought for refuge.

Sassacus and forty of his braves went to the Mohawks on the Hudson. Their treacherous hosts sent their heads back to the Englishmen.

The surviving Pequots offered to give up in order to save their lives from their enemies. Two hundred surrendered at Hartford. Uncas was given eighty, Miantonimoh of the Narragansett seventy and another chief twenty, never to live in their own land again. Those captured during the fighting were made slaves. So died the Pequot nation.

After this war, the Narragansett, jealous of the status Uncas now had with the whites, marched into Mohegan land with a thousand warriors. Uncas hurriedly rallied five hundred men and met Miantonimoh offering to fight him one on one to resolve the issue. The Narragansett, assured of their superior number, refused. At his haughty answer, Uncas fell face down on the ground. This was followed by a wall of arrows from the Mohegans who then charged. The Narragansett panicked and ran, their chief soon captured.

Uncas turned him in at Hartford, not wanting to take the life of such a great king. The council sent the captive to Boston for their decision. Five ministers were consulted after a failed vote and the decision was for him to be delivered to Uncas for execution. Two white men were sent with him to see that he was not tortured.

In single file the party moved through the forest with Uncas in the lead. At a sign from his chief, the man behind Miantonimoh delivered the death blow with his tomahawk, the prisoner never knowing what hit him. Uncas turned and carved out a chunk of the fallen chief's shoulder and put the bloody meat to his mouth, declaring it most delicious.

So ended the most dangerous Indian war to date. One race and their Indian allies the victors, the other annihilated.

# King Phillip's War

*Isolation* - that is the word that defined the plight of the New England colonies some forty years after the Pequot War. To protect themselves from outside enemies such as Indians, French and Dutch, on May 19, 1643, the New England Union was established.

This military alliance included Massachusetts Bay Colony, Plymouth Colony, Connecticut and New Haven. It's primary purpose was to offer a united military defense against the Dutch and Indians and to unit the church.

"Whereas we all came into these parts of America with one and the same end and aim, namely, to advance the Kingdom of our Lord Jesus Christ and to enjoy the liberties of the Gospel in purity with peace; and whereas in our settling (by a wise providence of God) we are further dispersed upon the sea coasts and rivers than was at first intended. . .

"And inasmuch as the natives have formerly committed sundry insolence and outrages upon several Plantations of the English and have of late combined themselves against us: . . . We therefore do conceive it our bounder duty, without delay to enter into a present consociation amongst ourselves, for mutual help and strength in all our future concerns: . . called by the name of the United Colonies of New England."

The Indians had retreated from the encroachment of the English settlers after the Pequot War.

New cabins struggled amongst the half-cleared fields and no roads connected the Connecticut River with the Hudson.

To the north lay treacherous mountains and dense forests reaching to the St. Lawrence River.

This isolation forged the New England character of independence, strong work ethics and high moral standards, intolerant of any infraction. Boston was the center of these colonies. Rough roads, in many places were only widened Indian trails, connected the center to the small incursions into the wilderness. Most only extended a few miles but some trails led all the way to the Connecticut River.

By 1675 clapboard homes of two stories had replaced the humble, rude cabins. Windows of paned glass and ground floors now encompassed three or four rooms with a commodious fireplace for cooking. It was a comfortable living inside that contrasted with the toil of fighting the wilderness on the outside.

Plymouth Colony had been overtaken with sand and the inhabitants were diminished in number. To the south lay Rhode Island and the prosperous city of Newport now under the control of the Quakers who had been driven out of Boston. Portsmouth was inhabited by the followers of another displaced Quaker, Mary Hutchison.

Massachusetts and Plymouth faced only broken remnants of tribes, weakened by disease and a holy fear of the Mohawks. Connecticut was protected by and lived hand in hand with Uncas, Chief of the Mohegans.

At the head of Narragansett Bay and the back door to Massachusetts lay Providence, Roger William's city containing 600 inhabitants. The nearby settlements of Warwick and old Rehoboth and scattered hamlets constituted what the Puritans called "a nest of pestilent heretics."

Providence Plantation and Rhode Island were the weak spot in the defense line with its divided sentiment and least organized government.

It was here at Providence that the New England Union met their most powerful and independent foes. Providence, isolated from the Union, faced the powerful Narragansett and their allies, the Wampanoags. Roger Williams in his friendship with the Narragansett had spent years dispelling hostilities caused mostly by his Puritan neighbors to the north.

Above the Connecticut River beyond the three major towns of Providence, Portsmouth and Newport lay Springfield, a town of 500. Seventeen miles north lay Northampton and across the river lay Hadley and then Hartford to the north of it.

Self-reliance was the way of life for these frontier settlers. The rich soil of the meadows and glades offered good pasturage to the livestock of the cabins' owners. Their humble dwellings clinging together for protection and comfort.

They were used to the occasional wigwam in the forest and the Indians they ran across seemed docile enough - the squaw with her baskets of corn, the warrior loafing, hunting, fishing and begging for a taste of the white man's firewater that was already ruining their civilization.

The United colonies probably had 30,000 to 40,000 inhabitants in 110 towns, 64 being in Massachusetts, with 6000 to 8000 able to bear arms.

Religion entered into their lives on a daily and personal level. They believed that God had given them the land from the Indians through purchase and trading. They felt they were a chosen people of God, having withstood religious persecution to survive here in the wilderness of North America. This present and personal God was fighting for them and if an opponent suffered, it was the wrath of God descending on him. How could they not look down at their Indian neighbors with such beliefs as these?

This thinking even hampers the Church today. They forgot that God in his mercy had saved them and not condemned them to the fires of hell. That God may also care for the savage did not occur to them. So when they went to combat, the slaughter of the Indians was divine judgment. While God was personally active, so was the Evil One. This lack of discernment drove them to acts that only the Evil One could create. Events they could not explain were attributed to the Evil One and these beliefs so sat the stage for this fierce war.

With their absorbing interest in religion, many men were concerned with the Indian's spiritual fate and worked hard to learn their languages and teach them the Gospel. Though it may have converted the simple Indian, it enraged the sachems (leaders) who could see that such teaching would diminish their influence.

The first such minister, John Eliot, who had learned the language and translated the Bible and other minor works, set up towns for the converts so that they could live civilized lives free from the lack of hygiene and morals of the Indians.

By the time the war broke out these contained 1150 praying Indians in fourteen towns in Massachusetts. Taking into consideration the other colonies, there were probably 4000 Indian converts (or semi-civilized Indians as some would suggest.)

The majority of those in these Indian towns quickly returned to the old ways at the first sign of trouble, though some had made true conversions and had learned to read and write. When war broke out, they were told to move to Deer Island in Boston harbor. 500 actually did, the rest disappearing into the forests.

Hunting bands of Indians slipped single file through the forests. The Indians had changed too. They now possessed finer weapons than the white settlers, procured from both Dutch and English traders and they had learned how to use them. They also knew that the time had come to drive out all the settlers if they were to have a chance to regain their land. But to understand the outcome, we must understand the individual Indian inside his culture.

The strength of the Indian was that of the hunter and the warriors were straight, tall and well-built whereas the women, through constant hard work and morale and mental suffering, were short, ungraceful and poor. The men exhibited great mental ability but were governed by their emotions and by superstitions, not by reason. In warfare they showed no generosity toward their foe. However, they never forgot a kindness or favor and were hospitable to friends and strangers. They were devoted fathers though the children thus produced were left to little discipline and much independence.

They dressed only in moccasins, small breeches of tanned deerskin fringed and embroidered with beads, the upper body left bare and greased. On the warpath the upper body was painted with grotesque designs and the totemic emblem of their clan on their breast. Their heads were shaved according to individual preference, all, half or all but the middle or a single tuft. Long mantles of multi- colored feathers were popular for the show-offs and skins were worn in the winter, fur side inward.

Spiritually, their gods dispensed good or evil fortune and every object had a spirit, inanimate as well as animate. They lived in clans and the clan took precedent over the whole. Each clan had its separate ward in the village and they marched together in war. To injure one was to injure all. This system exalted the individual in a closely knit democracy where insults were never borne. The superior air and attitude displayed by the Englishman stung the Indian to revenge the insult. What better means to starting a war?

***

So let us commence the tale of a war that proved most horrible and fierce, a war that set the New England colonies back at least fifty years in their progress and growth. A war that would result in the end of the Indian culture in New England.

By now their numbers had been reduced by disease to about ten thousand throughout all of New England.

Along the east coast of the Narragansett Bay lay the one thousand Wampanoags, Chief Massosoit's old tribe, reduced by disease to about five hundred warriors.

Along the west shore extending to the Pawcatuck River were four thousand Narragansett with one thousand warriors. Between the Connecticut River and the Thames lay one thousand Mohegans under Uncas who could furnish two hundred fighting men. From Northfield extending south and east into Connecticut were numerous villages of various tribes totaling five thousand which could furnish one thousand warriors. They all spoke a version of the Algonquian language.

The economic relationship between the Indians and whites can be traced to the rise and fall of the value of wampum (a quantity of small cylindrical beads made by North American Indians from qua-hog shells, strung together and worn as a decorative belt or other decoration or used as money).

Thirty years after Plymouth it was the legal tender of the area. The fur trade fell in 1662 and was replaced by the fishing industry. With it came silver coin exchanged in the West Indies and Europe for the fish. This depressed the value of wampum and the necessity to trade with the Indians. The Indian had profited by the trade but was now dependent on the white man's gun and the white man's blanket. In addition, he had become paralyzed by the strong water (liquor) of the white man.

The colonists derived their lands through just dealings of sale. But the Indians did not understand the right of possession. They did not understand that once they sold land, they could not use it. He gave his land away lavishly necessitating that the deeds be written in a conservative manner so as to protect the Indian's use until no longer needed. This does not dispel the fact that the New Englanders were land hungry. The Indian little appreciated the value of land until he needed it. So land and its use and possession became the catalyst to war as it always has.

Old Chief Massosoit of the Plymouth Colony treaty had lived a long peaceful life, dying about 1660. He had two sons, Wamsutta and Metacomet, he had given English names, Alexander and Philip.

Alexander, the elder, took over and married a

strong, influential woman named Wetamoo who was also a sachem. This alarmed the Plymouth colony who requested his presence at council. When he did not show up, Major Josiah Winslow, the son of Governor Edward Winslow of Plymouth colony, was instructed to arrest him which he did at gunpoint.

This enraged the young chief. While in custody at Winslow's home in Marshfield, seventeen miles north of Plymouth, he contracted a fever and pleaded to be allowed to go home for treatment.

He was released but died before he could get far. His squaw proclaimed the English had poisoned him.

Philip now became sachem of the Wampanoags. Conciliation on the part of the Plymouth Council might have won his good will, but he was constantly the object of Plymouth's suspicion for they knew Philip would not likely forget his brother's death. He was frequently summoned to Plymouth Council and forced to submit to various treaties. This treatment only increased his resentment and mistrust.

In 1674, a praying Indian named John Sausaman was killed. Because of a minor infraction he had left the civilized Indian town of Natick, 32 miles east of Boston, where he was a schoolmaster and joined Philip's service and as Philip's secretary learned his secrets. When he returned to Natick after satisfying the authorities of his change of heart, he revealed Philip's plot to confederate with neighboring tribes to attack the colony. He was soon murdered.

Tobias, one of Philip's counselors, was suspected and a witness claimed to have seen the murder at the hands of Tobias and two of his followers. The men were taken to Plymouth, tried and hung. This trial and execution turned the Wampanoags to revenge. Reports from farmers came in from far and wide of cattle shot in the field, corn stolen, houses broken into and pilfered. Strange Indians swarmed into Philip's camp who was sending his women and children to the Narragansett. Terror filled the valleys and farms waiting for the next aggressive attack.

In the spring of 1675, Captain Benjamin Church who was clearing a plantation heard rumors of Philip's attempt to confederate with a local squaw sachem, Awashonks, and secure her followers to his cause.

He went to meet with her. He found six hundred Indians in attendance at the festivities along with six of Philip's envoys. When asked by the Mount Hope Indian queen what she should do, he told her to kill the six messengers and ask for the protection of the Plymouth colony. Over the protests of some of her followers at this suggestion, he fearlessly told her that they were bloody wretches and not to be followed. She concurred and asked him to go to Plymouth on her behalf.

On his trip to Plymouth he met Queen Wetamoo of the Pocassets, the widow of Alexander, who told him she also had been approached by Philip's envoys. Initially she hesitated but the wily Philip convinced her to throw in her three hundred braves with his.

The following Sunday while the people of Swansea, Massachusetts were at church, young warriors came and pillaged their homes. Word was sent to Plymouth and Boston and orders were transmitted to the commanders of all the towns in the district to assemble their fighting men at Taunton, thirty-seven miles south of Boston and twenty-four miles east of Plymouth. Captain Church arrived from Plymouth with twenty horsemen.

The next Sunday the assembled forces asked for God's providential hand to turn aside the impending war.

Returning from church the settlers of Swansea, which was located fourteen miles southwest of Taunton, were fired upon, killing three and wounding one. In another part of town six more settlers were killed and their bodies horribly mutilated. War had come to New England after more than 40 years of peace.

The Boston council ordered troops to immediately prepare for war. A messenger they sent to reason with Philip at Mount Hope peninsula turned back at Swansea on discovering two bodies in the road.

The Boston forces marched at once, a company of foot soldiers and a company of horsemen. Each infantryman carried a musket and long knife fitted to affix to the muzzle, a knapsack with six feet of fuse, a pound of powder and a bandoleer passing under the left arm containing a dozen or more cylinders holding a measured charge of powder, a bag containing three pounds of bullets and a horn of priming powder. Fitness was a requirement for being an infantryman. The horsemen carried a carbine or two pistols and a sword. Their arrival at Swansea brought the force to 250.

Philip, driven into a conflict by emotions he could no longer control, knew his warriors desires for war and hoped Captain Benjamin Church, Father of the American Rangers success on his part would bring more followers. Yet, he also knew in his heart that he could rely only on his personal followers if things became bad. The time was ripe for a war and he had the advantage of knowing the fording places, the trails and the habits of the settlers. His men handled firearms well and knew how to turn every cover to their advantage, to strike when unexpected and flee rapidly into the impenetrable forest.

The forty years of peace had left the colonist soft and unprepared for war. The spread-out settlements would be easy targets for his fast-moving warriors.

What he forgot was that though the settlers lacked training, there were among them the officers of Cromwell's army, the most perfect army in the whole world. Materials were in abundance and the settlers knew and understood the Indian ways.

Many Indians would join them including all of the Mohegans. Philip had probably thirty-five hundred warriors - five hundred Wampanoags, eleven hundred from Nipmucks and Connecticut tribes, six hundred Abenakis and Tarratines, one thousand Narragansett and three hundred scattered warriors in other tribes. Because they could move fast, forty miles a day, their effect far exceeded their actual numbers.

Panic reigned among the far flung settlers who fled their homes for safety. On June 29th the Boston detachment reinforced the force at Swansea, bringing it to a total of five hundred, Major James Cudworth in command.

The army set out the next day to find Philip's main camp. They found empty wigwams and the smoking ruins of settlers' homes, torn Bibles, ghastly heads and hands of the occupants sticking up from the ground. Philip's wigwam was discovered and tracks led to the river. Evidently, he had left Mount Hope which was exactly a mile east of Warren, Rhode Island.

The force sought to contact the Narragansett in order to secure their alliance in the fight against Philip. They found a few old men and women who had come out of the swamps, who were forced to sign a treaty at gunpoint after a four day conference, agreeing to "give up, living or dead, any of Philip's subjects who should take refuge with them and to kill and to destroy to the best of their ability any of said enemy." Unfortunately, no important sachem had signed this treaty and the Narragansett felt that they had to bear another wrong." They considered the conduct of the colonies against them as aggressive and high-handed and many times unjust. Their present chief, the bold and war-like Canonchet, resented the treatment of his people.

Philip had taken refuge in wooded swamps and thickets of the Pocasset territory. Indians along the eastern shore of Mount Hope Bay had been forced to join him and war parties sallied forth, burning farms, shooting settlers from ambush and killing livestock.

Middleboro, five miles north of Taunton, was destroyed and the occupants forced to take refuge in a mill on the Nemasket River.

Captain Church with Captain Fuller was dispatched from Mount Hope to find the Indians who were already striking elsewhere and also to give aid to Awashonks on Mount Hope who had allied herself with Plymouth.

Church pro- posed a split march in quest of the enemy, taking nineteen volunteers from their thirty-six men. When Church was turned back in the search along the Bay, the sachem queen was forced to throw in with Philip's warriors out of protection.

Searching deep into the area toward Sankonett, twenty-one miles to the south, they were fired on by fifty or sixty muskets. Church looked behind himself expecting to see half of his company dead.

Instead, they were standing and firing briskly toward the smoke of the Indian guns.

Casting his eyes to the hill above, it seemed to move with the sun glittering on the Indians' gun barrels. In desperation he searched about for signs of the boats that were to have attended his force off of the bay. Unknown to him, the force now at Sandy Point across Mount Hope River had landed but was driven back into a fortified position with many wounded.

So that the New Englanders on the opposite shore would know them to be friends, he had the soldiers strip to their white shirts and fired a three gun signal. The men ran to a hedge row and all tumbled over down to the bank except one who was feared killed. In fact, the young man had fallen only to give himself time to place a bullet into one of his enemies' forehead and soon joined his company.

A boat sent across to aid them was driven back and the Indians knew they had their prey who would soon run out of ammunition. Church exhorted his men of God's provision in aiding them to this point and that He would continue to do so.

To prove his point, a sloop soon appeared on the river coming to their aid. Captain Roger Golding was a man of determination and sent them a canoe ashore while the Indians filled his sails, colors and stern full of bullet holes. Two men at a time were rowed to the ship and thus spared. Two days later, Captain Fuller's company was also retrieved, having received two men wounded. Both companies then returned to the fort at Mount Hope.

Major Cudworth and his men had moved toward Taunton to protect that side of the country from the attackers.

Upon learning of Philip's location in the cedar swamps of Pocasset, the force, now recombined and moved on his camp. Entering the swamp they were met with a fearsome volley that killed six men. The savages affixed bushes to their sides and were able to move about in the brush undetected and lured their pursuers deeper into the swamp which was located on the Taunton River directly opposite Somerset, Massachusetts.

Thinking Philip was finally cornered, the main army now disbanded, marching back to Boston leaving only one hundred men to build a fort and finish the war. They failed to reckon the cunning of their opponent. Quietly in the night he and his fighting men crossed the Taunton River on drift wood. All that was left for capture were women, children and the sick.

Crossing the plains at Rehoboth, eight miles north of Swansea, his force was met by fifty Mohegans and local forces that were reinforced from Swansea and Mount Hope. As night came on they paused in their pursuit. At dawn they overtook the Indians finding only Wetamoo's camp.

Following hard on Philip's heels, they were suddenly confronted by his fighting men. After a fierce fight which killed many on both sides, Philip withdrew.

The Mohegans, distracted by the plunder of the camp, could no long be compelled to fight. Captain Daniel Henchman who had come up from his fort at Pocasset did not pursue Philip aggressively and turn him back toward Mount Hope as he should have. He pursued in a leisurely manner until his supplies were used up leaving the western shore settlers to death by the tomahawk and scalping knife of the Nipmucks who were already rising.

Negotiations with the Indians left at Pocasset compelled one hundred and sixty to surrender. Despite the protestations of the captains who had captured them and taken them to Plymouth, they were sold into slavery.

As the Massachusetts Bay Colony and Plymouth hesitated in blindness, the Connecticut colony prepared for all out war. All Connecticut towns were ordered to prepare for defense.

The Mohegans donned their war paint with promises of reward for each scalp and prisoner taken. Connecticut realized the value of the Mohegan scouts while Massachusetts judged all Indians as treacherous. This helped the colony escape the bitterness of burned villages and slain settlers because they included the Mohegans with all of their expeditions. Uncas was still alive and as wily as ever and his braves did not much distinguish between Narragansett or Wampanoag scalps.

51

While destruction and war prevailed in the Rhode Island colony and Plymouth, and Connecticut lay safe, the western Bay settlements and the Connecticut Valley made no effort to prepare, confident of the Nipmucks' neutrality.

Some fifty miles to the north of Rehoboth, the Nipmucks led by Matoonas fell upon Mendon, Massachusetts. This news caused widespread fear since it was now evident that the war included more than one tribe.

The governor of Massachusetts dispatched an envoy, Ephraim Curtis, of Worcester, a notable hunter and scout well versed in the ways of the Indians. He sought a to reconcile with the Nipmucks and also to spy out the land. Curtis made three separate visits to the area. Outside Brookfield, Massachusetts some forty miles to the west of Mendon, he began efforts at a peace treaty.

A local farmer, Captain Hutchison with twenty horsemen under Captain Thomas Wheeler, commander of the militia from Concord met with an ambush that sent the negotiating party back with eight dead and many wounded. Ambushes all along the roads they had taken were avoided by the skillful scouting of two Praying Indians that took them back through another route. Sadly, these men through harsh treatment were later driven to join the enemy.

The settlement of only twenty houses had as its strongest house that of Sergeant John Ayres. Fifty women and children and thirty-two men huddled together there waiting for the next attack. Volley after volley of bullets hit the walls like hail and the smell of burning houses assailed the occupants' lungs. Men from inside were exposed to danger as they attempted to put out the fire the Indians had made around the stronghold. They exhorted one another in a loud voice, "God is with us and fights for us and will deliver us out of the hands of the heathen."

The Indians scoffed back, "Now see how your God will deliver you" as they sent shots into the groups of men.

God answered their prayers and only two men were wounded while the firing from the settlers killed many a foe.

After a third attempt to escape and get help, Curtis succeeded in crawling on his belly and eluding the surrounding enemy. He set out for Marlboro over 47 miles away. Inside, his companions not knowing his fate awaited theirs, vowing to send many a Nipmuck to the next world before they were killed. There was no lull in the fighting with the Indians pouring great amounts of shot into the structure with its foot thick walls. Though the bullets occasionally penetrated the walls, they inflicted little casualties - only two who were foolish enough to look outside or venture out were killed. One woman was killed by a bullet that entered a loophole.

Gathered at the nearby church, the "howling

hounds of hell" scoffed and made hideous attempts at hymns, having been joined evidently by some Praying Indians who no longer had their restraints. The settlers fired fiercely on this assembly and had the satisfaction of seeing many carried off.

The trapped inhabitants watched all day as the numbers of attackers swelled and the attempts to burn them out increased. Arrows with fiery rags hit the roof. The men inside cut away the shingles to extinguish the flames. Hay and flax against the out-side walls were set aflame, the attackers standing close to shoot down any one who attempted to put out the inferno. God sent a downpour in answer to prayer of the trapped settlers.

Judah Trumble traveling on his way home to Springfield saw the flames, crept up to the be-sieged town and then fled to get help. Messengers were sent to Hartford and Boston and warnings sent to the settlements through the area. A force from Springfield reinforced by Mohegans set out.

Another force commanded by Major Simon Wil-lard, a 70 year-old patriarch that had been dis-patched to Groton, on hearing the news, turned aside to Brookfield. His forty-six men marched into the garrison and the Indians withdrew after setting fire to the remaining buildings. It was estimated that 80 Indians had been killed in the defense of the little settlement. Probably induced by the stress of the attacks, two pairs of twins were born to the women inside the fortress during the siege.

Reinforcements now poured in bringing Major Willard's force up to 350. They scoured the area but with little success and had no idea where or when the next blow would fall. The Connecticut Valley was evidently in danger. Hadley, a settlement 31 miles further up the Valley, was picked as a stockade and Brookfield was soon abandoned.

Deerfield, twenty-one miles north of Hadley with a population of one hundred twenty-five, was burned to the ground and Northfield, another town fifteen miles up river from Deerfield, came under hostile guns of the Pocumtucks led by Sagamore Sam and "One- eyed John". Nine or ten more settlers were killed before they could reach the garrison town.

Reinforcements sent out from Hadley under Captain Richard Beers before knowledge of their fate was known were ambushed, killing twenty of the thirty-six men.

Several were captured and one, Robert Pepper, survived to meet Mrs. Rowlandson during her captivity. He reported he was not treated unkindly due to the intervention of Sagamore Sam.

It was estimated that almost one hundred and twenty warriors took part in this attack. A small guard left with the horses stumbled back to Hatfield with the terrible news.

Two days later one hundred men under Major Robert Treat, commander-in-chief of the Connecticut military forces and later governor of Connecticut, came out to find a ghastly site at the battleground - the heads of their comrades including Captain Beers', stuck on poles and a body suspended from a pole by a hook in its lower jaw. The relief party, knowing all too well the cruelty of the red men, suspected the prisoner had been alive when so suspended. While burying their dead they were fired upon. Services suspended, the town was abandoned. They marched away leaving all but their horses and a few cattle, the Indians soon burned the once flourishing settlement.

When Deerfield had been abandoned, Three thousand bushels of grain had been left behind.

On September 18, with winter coming on, Captain Thomas Lothrop, with 80 men recruited from Essex County, was dispatched to bring it in. Having learned nothing from recent events, no scouts were sent out and some of the men laid down their guns to gather wild grapes. A huge force of Pocumtucks, Nonatucks, Nashaways and Squakheags under Sagamore Sam, "One-eyed John", Muttaump and possibly Philip lay in wait for the expedition. It was the saddest day in the early history of New England when one thousand warriors pounced upon the unsuspecting teamsters and their escorts. The ambush, known as the Battle of Bloody Brook, killed all but 9 by nightfall. The survivors met the savages with their own methods, hiding behind trees and fighting to the end. Seventeen teamsters from Deerfield (half of the adult male population of that town) and forty-three young men from Essex County perished.

Captain Moseley, on a scouting expedition nearby, came to their aid with seventy men but too late to save them. The attackers, many of them Christian Indians, shouted to him. "Come on Moseley, Come On. You want Indians. Here are enough Indians for you." He lost eleven of his men killed. His force, skillfully employed, fought the Indians for a full day.

At nightfall Major Treat with one hundred whites and Mohegans came to their relief lest they also perish. Retreating to Deerfield, they returned the next day, which was the Sabbath, to bury the dead, seventy-one in a mass grave.

Too everyone's astonishment, it was while they were busy at this gruesome work, one of the slain stood and staggered toward them. He had been shot in the head, scalped, stripped, and lain naked all night. He survived to live years afterward.

This company of the most prominent men of the county left many a widow and child to mourn. One plantation alone left eight widows and twenty-six children orphaned. The real fault that allowed all these massacres was the commanders' failure to keep the simplest precautions against surprise attacks. This failure would reap even more English blood in the French and Indian Wars almost a century later.

Deerfield was doomed. On the frontier law had been loosely enforced and perpetrators of aggressions against the Indians had not been prosecuted. Local Indians had been kidnapped and sold into slavery, abused, raped and plundered. No wonder the local Indians looked on the English commanders with suspicion. An Indian never forgets an insult. Now was the time for all Indians to remember their grievances and strike.

These successful missions encouraged the Indians into attacking more strongly fortified towns as the war spread. Twenty-seven men left to guard Deerfield watched in dismay as hundreds of the attackers paraded in the field before them in clothing they had taken off of the dead. The bold leader in the garrison sounded a trumpet which forced the Indians to flee in fear of a large force inside.

No respite was coming and Deerfield had to be abandoned, leaving the whole valley a wasteland.

Hadley was now in a state of fear, fueled by the thought of ambush into which almost every force had marched The constant need to watch for foe and the sight of disembodied heads and decomposing bodies in the meadows.

These vicious attacks turned the public feeling in New England to an indiscriminate hatred of all Indians. To be an Indian, whether innocent or not, was to be condemned. Many Praying Indians were falsely accused by other Indians and tried under less than civil law. Some were set upon when attempting to parley for treaties.

Meanwhile, the ministers of New England looked

upon these attacks as coming from God who was provoked because of the sins of the colonies. Clergy in Boston issued the following decree:

> "Some course should be undertaken for the suppression of those proud excesses in apparel, hair . . . That a due testimony should be borne against such as false worshipers, especially such as idolatrous Quakers, who set up altars against the Lord's altars, yea who set up a Christ whom the Scriptures know not."

Other sins enumerated included drunkenness, swearing profanely, lax observation of the fourth and fifth commandments, oppression by merchants of day laborers, and Indian trading houses that had debauched the Indians with liquor. Further more care should be taken to the rising generation that they might be brought under the discipline of Christ.

Plymouth was more practical in its recommendations: everyone coming to meeting must be armed, no unnecessary shooting except at Indians or wolves. This was because ammunition was scarce in Plymouth.

Western Massachusetts passed resolutions of a different nature. At Springfield thirty-four miles south of Deerfield, the local Indians had been friendly, but in light of the spreading war, were no longer to be trusted. A plot to attack the town was uncovered by a friendly Indian and a warning was sent to the settlers. The people took refuge immediately in the garrison houses. Their leader, Lieutenant Cooper, and a companion ventured out to reconnoiter the Indian fort nearby. He was shot and his companion killed. Unable to return to Springfield with his wound, he sought the nearest garrison house where he died. Now without a leader, the people inside Springfield fought back the ensuing attacks until help arrived under Major Pynchon, son of the founder of Springfield and commander of the entire army in the Connecticut Valley.

Coming from Hadley returned to a terrible home-coming. Thirty-two houses, twenty-five barns, grist mills, libraries, burnt to the ground leaving forty families destitute. Only thirteen houses survived. Three settlers had been killed. The only Indian captured, an old squaw, was ordered torn to pieces by dogs. Seems the English could be just as barbaric as their enemy.

This burning of Springfield renewed the Indian passions for more. Brookfield had been the only settlement in central Massachusetts. All the towns along the frontier were now in danger.

Moseley and other commanders felt it a waste of time to leave towns under-garrisoned while forces scoured the land for Indians they never found leaving the towns unprotected. All operations in the field were suspended for weeks with only a contingent left at Deerfield and Springfield. Connecticut recalled their troops under Major Treat on fear of an attack on Glastonbury, leaving the forces under

United Colony command depleted.

With the removal of the forces opposing them, the Indian aggressors went on the offensive again. On October 19th, Hatfield was attacked, the Indians setting fire to the woods north of town. A ten man squad sent out to determine the cause were shot down, six killed and three captured, only one escaping back to the garrison.

Captain Samuel Appleton from Hadley arrived with reinforcements before the main attack came. The force inside fought fiercely and the Indians were driven off after a great slaughter to their numbers and the appearance of Major Treat who had returned.

Because of this the hostiles ceased to attack anymore towns the rest of that year. The main body withdrew for the winter to the country of the Narragansett.

As the snow enclosed the surviving settlements, the survivors thanked God for his protection sent in this manner. However, they had to watch as the Indians availed themselves of their crops left in the fields, while they wondered how they would stave off starvation.

The people took the opportunity along with the assistance of the soldiers among them to erect strong eight foot high stockades around their towns. They lived together in few houses with little comfort. However, when they thought of those buried under the frozen soil, they realized their life was the greatest reward and thanked God for it.

Appleton, who had taken over command when Moseley resigned, left a small garrison at Hadley, Northampton and Springfield. He marched back to Boston to prepare for a war against the Narragansett.

The Connecticut Valley campaign had been a dismal failure due to conflicting commands from the Council, the lack of agreement and no definite plan of operation. They had always been on the defensive, drawn out to hunt for a vanishing foe they never found and then been ambushed by that same foe at every unexpected opportunity.

The Indians, their crops gone and their weapons diminished, wandered away in search of sustenance.

The New Englanders were now aroused to act in a spirit of vengeance. The war had become a racial and religious divide. Repressive measures were popular and the pleas for humane treatment by those leaders who knew it was great folly fell on deaf ears.

These harsh measures cost Massachusetts dear. It left her forces helpless to carry on a successful campaign without the aid of friendly Indians. Connecticut which took a less condemning view and used the Mohegans to their advantage suffered little.

For some time the usual suspicious relationships between the whites and the Narragansett had simmered below the surface. Rumor charged they had given shelter to the women and children of the Wampanoags. (Uncas was more than willing to spread such rumors to his advantage.)

The treaty with them, wrung at sword point, was useless. In addition they had refused, as they had promised earlier in the year, to turn over Wetamoo who was seeking shelter with them.

The Council decided to strike first in winter while they were in camp. The Rhode Islanders led by Roger Williams, ever a friend to the Narragansett, opposed this action to no avail. The heretical Rhode Islanders were ignored even though the Narragansett lay within their boundaries and invasion violated the Rhode Island charter which stated that it was unlawful for the rest of the Colones to invade or molest Native Indians.

The 2nd day of December was set aside for humiliation and prayer. By the 8th the forces were organized at Dedham, Massachusetts eleven miles southwest of Boston. Connecticut sent three hundred and fifteen men under Major Treat with one hundred and fifty Pequot and Mohegans as auxiliaries. Massachusetts provided a four hundred and sixty-five foot soldiers, two hundred and seventy-five horses besides volunteers, teamsters and servants with Governor Winslow of Plymouth in command.

Historians declare Winslow to have been a man of courage, resolution, determination and prudence.

One hundred and fifty-eight men of Plymouth under Major William Bradford joined the force at Providence, Rhode Island.

Captain Church whom you may remember from earlier had arrived before them and in his normal aggressive manner led some friends out into the night. Next morning they returned to greet the commander of the Plymouth troops with eighteen prisoners.

On the 9th they marched and Moseley immediately ran into thirty-six Narragansett Indians including one called Peter who had been insulted by a fellow countryman. In revenge he turned traitor and led them to the winter camp.

Ten years later Peter received the monetary reward he had been promised and his daughter who had been captured and sold as a slave was found and returned to him.

By the 13th all forces had assembled at Smith's Landing near Wickford waiting for the Connecticut troops to arrive, having marched some 60 miles since the 9th. After a Narragansett ambassador who was suspected of being a spy was sent away on the 15th, considerable numbers of Narragansett hovered around the camp firing into it indiscriminately killing several men.

On the 17th at Tower Hill eight miles away seventeen careless soldiers were slaughtered as they slept in a stone mill. All colonial troops had assembled by the 18th after several minor skirmishes that left several dead on both sides; the main attack was ordered for the next morning.

Their goal, the fortified winter camp of the Narragansett, lay sixteen miles to the west situated in a cedar swamp. It was situated near the present town of South Kingston, Rhode Island about forty miles south of Providence. Here many warriors with women and children resided in bark wigwams lined with skins and heavily stocked with winter supplies of corn and dried fish. It had been fortified which was atypical of the Indians.

A strong stockade ringed the camp which was backed with ramparts of rocks and clay and numerous blockhouses and flankers to protect the entrance to the village - a most formidable structure indeed, buried in the middle of a swamp passable by only a single trail. Outside the stockade, trees had been felled with their tops pointing upward. The single entrance was along the trunk of a lone tree.

Thus begun the Great Swamp Fight on December 16, 1675. After the march in bitter cold without food, with frozen hands and feet, the United Colony Army, the largest ever assembled in the colonies, reached the fort.

The frozen swamp made the access easy enough though the attackers saw at once the weak spot in the formidable fortifications, a corner obstructed by a single log. To this the New Eng landers attacked. The first volley from the Narragansett killed a large number of three companies of Massachusetts troops that fell back. Reinforced they surged forward only to have more of their ranks thinned including three of their officers.

Only when the Connecticut troops rushed to their aid despite the blinding fire was progress made, at the sacrifice of three more officers. Foot by foot the Englishmen forced the Indians back despite severe losses on all sides as the Narragansett fought from behind wigwams and baskets of corn.

The always active Captain Church swept into the village over the bodies of his captains. The retreating Indians took to the swamp and he pursued. The Narragansett had not given up. They were the most warlike of the tribes and now it was a fight to the death.

Even the Mohegans feared them and had refused to join this attack, fearing recriminations if the Englishmen should fail. Seeing that he had gone too far and was now cut off, Church commanded his men to lie down and prepare their weapons to repulse a counterattack of the Indians who were forming behind the stockade.

Allowing the Indians to group themselves, as they rose to move forward his men fired on them from the rear and they ran in panic, some going back into the stockade. Church was wounded in the ensuing battle.

When the fighting had died down, the men prepared to torch the wigwams. Church protested explaining that the wounded could be cared for inside them as they were lined with baskets of corn and would be protection against the cold. Winslow tended to agree but was over-ruled by his captains who feared being caught inside.

So the dreary march back began with one hundred and seventy wounded, leaving behind six officers and twenty men who had been killed. Their march was lighted by the fire of the burning village.

It was a most terrible journey through blowing snow. Twenty-two of the wounded died during the march. They finally reached Wickford at 2 in the morning, with many having lost their way.

Winslow with forty men did not reach camp until 7 in the morning. They now had over 85 fatalities as more wounded died.

On top of this, snow began to fall in even greater volume so that travel was impossible for weeks on end. However, a ship with provisions arrived that same day from Boston.

The Indian dead were not counted but reports varied from as few as forty-five warriors and three hundred old men. The women and children as given by Narragansett themselves, to ninety-eight killed and forty-eight wounded besides the women and children. This was given by a renegade Englishman who had been in the compound as a traitor and had been seen to fight against his countrymen, something for which he was later hanged.

Others exaggerated the Indian losses to as high as

a thousand killed, besides the women and children.

Their provisions for winter had been destroyed and they had been driven out into the woods to face starvation. However, they were not destroyed by any means.

The Connecticut troops were so destroyed that Major Treat had to take them home and recruit more soldiers. The wounded were sent to Providence and other cities for care. The remainder dug in until an unexpected thaw allowed reinforcements of three hundred men from Connecticut to arrive in January bringing the force to fourteen hundred.

On Jan. 27, 1676 they went out in search of their opponent who had already attacked Warwick, Rhode Island twenty-four miles to the north and twelve miles south of Providence. It was later abandoned, finding many a burned house and over sixty remains of horses that had been consumed.

They overtook the Indian rear guard killing seventy. The main body could not be cornered for at the first sight of white men, they would disappear into impenetrable swamps.

Thus begun the "hungry march" of the colonial army. Here and there they found a few women and children and burned a few wigwams. In the early part of February on reaching Marlboro, thirty miles west of Boston, the troops had to give up the pursuit when their provisions ran out. They were disbanded on Feb. 3, a grave mistake. All it had done was spread the war over a wider area.

Marlboro was strategically located being on the Connecticut trail and the last town before the Connecticut Valley. The occupants expected it to be the first town to be attacked in the spring.

Philip, the instigator of all this trouble, now took himself and his followers to a winter camp some twenty miles northeast of Albany, New York where he could communicate with the French and Mohawks and trade with the Dutch. His followers had been depleted even more by disease in the previous months than those lost in the war, but yet he sought to fight. He vowed "to live as long as we can and die like men and not live to be enslaved."

The winter brought great sufferings among all the Indians, as the war had prevented the tribes in the Connecticut Valley from harvesting their corn. Now they were sought by Wampanoags and Narragansett who had poured in from the battlefields. Raids on English villages became necessary for the procurement of food.

To fight these attacks, the colonists needed information, so two Praying Indians were chosen from those taking refuge on Deer Island, James Quannapohit and Jacob Kattenanit. These men proved invaluable to the service of the English army acting as spies and messengers as needed.

James was a scout of great skill and bravery. He was marked by Philip for assassination because of his friendship with the English. They were secretly brought away and set behind English lines. They found that the Wampanoags were very pleased that they now had such a powerful tribe as the Narragansett as allies.

The word was they planned to burn Lancaster, which lay fourteen miles to the northwest of Malboro. The stalwart Quannapohit, came in quite worn out from traveling great distances on snow shoes to warn them on Jan. 24 and Minister Rowlandson had left immediately for Boston to beg for adequate protection. On February 8th new recruits of six hundred men were summoned, but before the army could assemble, Lancaster, some thirty miles west of Boston became the next target.

Jacob had stayed behind when James Quannapohit had left because his three children were held captive and he wanted to try and gain their release.

The whole frontier to the east was at the mercy of the Indians who quickly attacked Lancaster, a village of some sixty families, on Feb. 10.

Jacob Kattenanit arrived breathless at Major Gookins' door on the night of the 9th, having traveled over eighty miles on snowshoes to warn them. Gookin immediately sent messengers for help but it was too late.

The garrison at Lancaster consisted of five fortified houses spread far apart. Inside the Rowlandson house thirty-seven men, women and children were awakened to the terrible cries from outside of their enemy. They watched in horror in the dim light of dawn as Indians burned the other houses and massacred the occupants with tomahawk and rifle. One begged on his knees and was killed with glee, his body stripped naked and his bowels ripped open. Soon most of the houses had been overrun but theirs. It was not a well-fortified position being on a hill and the rear loopholes obscured with wood stacked for the winter. After a fight of over two hours during which one after another of the occupants were killed, the Indians set fire to the house. The survivors rushed out in hopes of reaching another garrison.

Only one man escaped and the women and children that were not killed were taken captive. Mrs. Rowlandson, the wife of the minister, was captured after twelve inside were killed and the others taken prisoner.

Captain Wadsworth arrived in time to the save the other garrisons but not those that had been killed and captured.

It was a solemn sight to see so many Christians lying in their own blood, all of them stripped naked by the howling hounds of hell. Among those were most of Mrs. Rowlandson's family: her sister and two of her sons killed, a son and three daughters captured. Her own child in her arms was wounded when a bullet passed through her side and through the child's bowels. The Indians carried her and her wounded child on horseback most of the journey, but fed her nothing for four days. Her little girl lived nine excruciating days, dying at age 6 years and 5 months.

She was sold by the Narragansett who captured her to Quinnopan, a sagamore married to King Philip's sister-in-law, Wetamoo. In the same village was her ten year-old daughter, Mary, who had been taken captive by a Praying Indian and sold for a gun.

She prayed for the knowledge of her sixteen year old son, Joseph, and God answered her prayer when he was allowed to come visit her from another village.

Another answer to prayer came after the Indians had attacked Medford and returned with many English scalps (23) but also an English Bible which one of the Indians offered to her. She was soon parted from Mary whom she did not see again until she was returned from captivity and four cousins and neighbors that she never saw again.

Later she learned that one woman who was pregnant and vexed the Indians with her begging to go home, was stripped naked as they danced about her in front of a fire; she and her daughter in her arms were then killed and their bodies thrown into the fire.

She spent six months running and starving with the Wampanoags as they evaded the colonial army.

For the most part she and the other captives were treated with kindness. She was eventually taken to King Philip's wigwam and offered a smoke. She had smoked before her captivity but was now ashamed to admit such a depraved habit. He asked her to make a shirt for his son and gave her a schilling in pay which her master allowed her to keep.

After that she mended the Indian childrens' clothes and made them articles of clothing thus proving her usefulness to the whole village.

Finally, her master prepared to take her for ransom back to her husband. Later the warriors attacked Hadley and brought back a captive, Thomas Read. He was weeping as he supposed they would kill him. She asked their captors if they would and they said no.

Their capriciousness seems so strange to the civilized mind, one minute being kind and offering someone food and comfort, the next scalping and doing unspeakable things to their enemies. Their emotional state was very much of the type known as devil possession. And yet, many Indians became Christians and stayed loyal to their Lord, some even paying with their lives in the fighting.

Eventually she was told she must go to her master at Wachuset because letters had come from the Union Council for the redeeming of the captives. On the three day journey she felt she would die before reaching the rendezvous. King Philip himself came up to her and took her hand saying, "Two weeks more and you shall be mistress again."

She was glad to see her master at Wachuset who brought water to her himself so that she could bathe. He gave her the looking glass so she could see how she looked and ordered his squaw to feed her. This is an old tactic for making the prisoner appear to be in better condition than they are in order to get a higher ransom.

It was here she learned that her master had three squaws, living with one at a time. The oldest one was kind and told her to come to her any time for food. Wetamoo, whom she had lived with, was proud and vain and jealous of the older woman, fearing she would loose some of the ransom to the older woman if she cared for the captive in her wigwam.

Then came the two Praying Indian scouts, Peter and Tom, with letters from the Council. On seeing them, though they be Indians, she burst into tears. The Grand Council of Indians called her to their wigwam and asked her how much her husband would pay for her. She knew her husband had lost all but did not want to insult them. So she said 20 pounds and that was the message sent to Boston. While she awaited the answer she found that her sister who had also been taken was nearby and begged to be allowed to see her, to no avail.

When the decision had been made to send her home, many Indians offered her gifts and shook her hand. One couple said they would run away with her if she wished to do so. She refused and waited for her release the next day. She was brought back to Lancaster with the Englishman who had been sent to retrieve her, Mr. John Hoar.

In dismay she saw the town in ashes. Upon

reaching Concord she met her brother and brother-in-law who asked of his wife. He had unknowingly buried her with the other burned bodies at the garrison house not knowing her body was among those unrecognized. She finally reached Boston and was reunited with her husband, both sorrowful at leaving their children still in the hands of the Indians though they were later released.

Concerning the treatment of captives, both parties could be cruel to the extreme. Torture of prisoners was the exception, not the rule and women and children were not tortured or killed but usually spared if the circumstances allowed. However, it must be pointed out that the enraged settlers slew without concern for women and children, an old European habit.

The previous generation had burned the women and children alive in the Pequot village, the present generation carried on this abomination and the future one would bring upon our history the Salem witch trials.

The thoughts of the colonists became merciless because of their belief that they were the new people of God and the Indians the Canaanites. Rhode Island alone prohibited the terrible practice of selling the captives into slavery in the West Indies.

Many Praying Indians stood firm for the Lord. Others turned their backs and participated in the fights, even betraying relatives into English hands to save themselves. During this time many of the

Praying Indians took part in the attack on Sudbury, seventeen miles to the east of Lancaster, killing over one hundred Englishmen.

The war's progress during the six months of Mrs. Rowlandson's captivity brought terrible losses to both sides. It had become a war of attrition. The same day as the attack on Lancaster in February, warriors also struck at Concord, twenty miles north-west of Boston.

Attacks came like a tidal wave over the towns and settlements of the frontier. No community, farm or trading post was safe. One-eyed John led a trail of blood through the forest toward the Plymouth colony. On Feb. 21st he struck Medfield, a town only twenty miles south of Boston, unwisely surrounded by fields of brush where timber had been cut down and brush allowed to flourish rather than crops. The force of one hundred and sixty soldiers were spread out amongst the populace and not congregated in a method to repel an attack of four hundred Indians.

The Indians torched all the homes at once and shot down the inhabitants as they exited in their bed clothes silhouetted against the flames. Twenty people were shot down on their thresholds. Many others were captured. A husband would flee with a child in one direction and a wife with a child in another. One would escape and the other would be killed or taken prisoner. One old man of 100 was burned alive in his home.

Forty or fifty homes were in flames as the survivors reached the garrison with its cannon and the solders prepared to give battle. As the Indians drew off, burning a bridge behind them, the troops in pursuit found the following notice attached to the post:

> "Know by this paper, that the Indians thou hast provoked to wrath and anger will war this 21 years if you will. There are many Indians yet. We come 300 at this time. You must consider the Indians lose nothing but their lives. You must lose your fair houses and cattle."

This was another bloody lesson that the New Englanders never seemed to learn, that the Indian fought by secretive ambush and attacks in the night. The old myth that Indians never attacked at night caused many a loss of life.

Town after town had been burned and here at Medfield, a guard of thirty men had allowed four hundred Indians to sneak past them.

A very important meeting took place on March 9 near Northfield, sixteen miles north of Deerfield on the Connecticut River.

Philip and Canonchet met in council with Quinnopan (Philip's cousin) who held Mrs. Rowlandson, and his wife Queen Wetamoo, Philip's chief leader, Annawan, and several chiefs of the Wampanoags, Pocumtucks, and Nipmucks.

Full of hope at their coming victory, within six months they would all be defeated in chains, killed by bul- let or the gallows. They needed seed to plant, land secure from attack and a safe place for the women and children. If they could attack fiercely in the east, this would distract the soldiers and leave the fertile ground between Deerfield and Northampton open for their use. This plan over-looked the effect of the friendly Indians and the perseverance of the settlers.

The plan nearly succeeded. Let us take a look at how it played out.

March brought terrible losses to the English all over New England. Groton, Massachusetts, thir-ty-five miles northwest of Boston, was attacked on March 2, the Indians rifling a few houses and stealing cattle. This was done as a large force of soldiers under Major Savage came from Quabaug, near Brookfield, to attack the Indian village situated amongst the swamps. Many hundred Indians, old, young, sick, lame and carrying papooses escaped as the ablest warriors drew the English off in trivial pursuit. Thus, they escaped across Miller's River in safety. Savage had been out-maneuvered.

Savage then marched to Hadley to join Turn-er. They were sent immediately to garrison at Northampton.

With Savage's return to the Connecticut Valley, the eastern frontier of the Bay settlements and area south of Plymouth and Narragansett Bay had no garrisons.

At Northampton the attackers broke through the

palisade. Unknown to them, the seventy-eight soldiers under Captain Turner had been reinforced with two hundred Connecticut men under Major Treat.

Once inside they were attacked by the well-garrisoned force and retreated, never attacking another palisaded town.

They lingered about waiting for people to stick their heads out of the garrisons at Hadley and Hatfield. Men slept on their muskets.

A few days later, Warwick, eleven miles south of Providence, was burned, leaving only one stone house upright. Wickford and Pawtuxet Rhode Island, in close proximity, came next.

The same day the council of chiefs was held, knowing the English were now long gone, some warriors returned to Warwick and waited for the appearance of the returning settlers. For the next few days they picked off the settlers by drawing them out of their garrisons and cutting them off.

When a command of soldiers came out to run them off, they drew them into an ambush, AGAIN.

Running for one of the four garrison houses, the defenders watched the Indians burn the whole town of forty homes.

The leader of these four hundred, One-eyed John, scoffed at the minister as they burned his meeting house and to Captain James Parker, the commander, he boasted of having burned Medfield and Lancaster and in a few days with his hundreds would do the same to Cambridge, Concord, Roxbury and Boston. His men, in a terrible show of psychological warfare, dug up the dead and displayed them to the beleaguered inside the garrison houses then withdrew in anticipation of a relief army coming upon them. A few days later the settlers guarded by soldier abandoned the town. Even then, two being picked off from ambush.

Throughout the Connecticut Valley, known as the breadbasket of New England with its thousands of acres of crops, and eastward to Providence and Plymouth, the war parties spread death and destruction. In Massachusetts Marlboro and Sudbury felt the shock of more attacks.

On Feb. 25 Weymouth, twenty miles south of Boston, was attacked. But it was Plymouth colony that bore the brunt of the worst fighting.

The Narragansett, returning to their homeland, sought revenge on their neighbors at Plymouth. On March 12 they surprised Clark's garrison on the Eel River. Founded in 1622 by Thomas Clark, a mate on the Mayflower, in lay one-half mile west of present day Chiltonville. Hiding until the men were at church next day, they fell upon the 11 women and children left behind and slew them all except Clark's son, Thomas, who survived a tomahawk strike to the skull. He was later tended by the famous Dr. John Clarke of Boston who inserted a silver plate into his skull. He was every after called "silver-headed Tom".

The reward for the attackers was handsome.

Seven muskets, thirty pounds of powder and one hundred fifty pounds in silver sterling. This was the closest the Indians got to Plymouth.

The towns around the Narragansett Bay were abandoned save for the soldiers. On March 14th the Wampanoags attacked and burned Rehoboth, leaving only two houses standing. Though only one man was killed when he naively refused to run for the garrison but, instead, had sat with a Bible in his lap, proclaiming to the Lord for his protection. The murderers ripped open his belly and stuck his Bible inside.

The next target, Providence, had been abandoned by its five hundred inhabitants who took refuge on an island. All though fifty to one hundred brave souls stayed to protect their possessions.

Good old Roger Williams, always a friend to the Indians, went out to meet the attackers. He was 77 years of age and ready to die. After warning them that England would continue to send men until they were wiped out, the savages replied, "Let them come. We are ready for them. But as for you, Roger Williams, you are a good man; you have been kind to us many years; not a hair of your head will be touched." However, the town was almost completely destroyed.

On March 17th the abandoned town of Warwick fell to the torch, as did the deserted homes of Simsbury, a plantation of forty homes covering seven miles in length along the Tunxis (Farmington) River.

Soldiers in garrisons could only watch the flames of homes and fields, while the displaced people prayed for deliverance from their enemies.

On March 26th the people of Marlboro sat in church in the middle of the town which had four garrisons, very spread out and hard to defend. It had been used constantly as a military post and Philip wanted it destroyed.

The Indians knew the devout worshipers would be in their houses of worship on Sunday and used this to plan their attacks when the people least expected them.

As God's plans would have it, the minister came down from his pulpit and walked about to relieve a toothache. In so doing he spied the Indian approach through the door and all ran for the garrison. One of their congregation was killed, as eleven barns and thirteen houses met the torch. That evening the lieutenant in command of the garrison found the Indians asleep around their campfire and dispatched four to the happy hunting grounds including the leader, Netus, who had attacked Sudbury.

On the same day sixty-three men and twenty Indians sent out from Plymouth under Captain Michael Pierce were caught in an ambush of five hundred warriors under Canonchet near Skeekonk, Massachusetts. Though a messenger was sent for help to Captain Edmunds at Providence, eight miles to the west, he foolishly refused to interrupt the church service to deliver the message and by then it was too late. All they could do when they reached the battlefield was bury the dead. Fifty-two Englishmen and eleven friendly Indians had been slain.

They had given up theirs lives dearly, killing one hundred and forty Indians in the attack. This was a tragedy to Plymouth colony. Some weeks later, nine men who had been captured were found murdered at Cumberland, Rhode Island, tomahawked and scalped. The word from the Indians was that these had been taken to be tortured but an argument about their fate had ensued and thus they were slain by the tomahawk.

On March 28th The victorious enemy then marched on Seekonk, a town built in a circular lay out. Every building except one was destroyed while those in the garrison in the center watched in helplessness.

On the same day at Springfield, sixty miles west of Marlboro, a group of church goers, eighteen men and a number of women and children, were attacked by seven Indians. After John Keep and a maid were killed, the soldiers ran off leaving behind Mrs. Keep, another woman and two children who were captured. So the ditty was composed, " Seven Indians and one without a gun, caused Captain Dixon and forty men to run".

When efforts were made to rescue them, the Indians struck them with the tomahawk. Mrs. Keep and the children died. The surviving woman said the attackers were Springfield Indians and had treated them kindly until pursued by the soldiers. She further said the Indians had been supplied with powder by Dutch traders and that there were three hundred Indians at Deerfield, three hundred above there and three hundred at Northfield.

Towns from Plymouth to northwest of Boston (Wrentham, Plymouth, Andover, Chelmsford, Scituate, Bridgewater and Middleboro) were all attacked. Some repelled the fiends, others suffered dearly. To the reader it is monotonous to read of one town ambushed after another. The slaughter of helpless men and women was a dreary fate in one settlement, then its neighbor. What would stop them? Who could stop them?

In desperation the Connecticut Council sent letters to Governor Andros of New York. Both sides in this correspondence were angry in their demands. Andros was reluctant to encourage the Mohawks to attack the valley tribes as the Connecticut Council asked. He wrote to the leaders inquiring if they would welcome the Mohawks among them in their towns and settlements and feed them? To their credit the Connecticut men knew this would be an inducement for the Mohawks to attack the Mohegans also, these allies being the main reason why the Connecticut settlements had not been attacked before. Andros did not intend to have the war spread into his territory. But the Mohawks did keep the valley Indians in fear and in March and April their warriors did attack the New England Indians encamped near the Hudson and drove them out of the area.

A break in the constant defeats at the hands of the Indians came on April 3rd when Canonchet took fifteen of his braves and set out to procure seed corn from Seekonk near his home on New Hope.

In the area was a force of Connecticut men under Captain George Dennison of Stonington, with seventy-nine soldiers and various Indians from the Niantics, Pequot, and Mohegans under Uncas' son, Oneko. Reaching the Pawtucket River, they came upon one of Canonchet's men with two squaws. The warrior was killed and the two squaws captured. To their surprise they informed Captain Dennison that Canonchet was near by. At that same moment their scouts returned reporting they had found Can- on- chet and some wigwams. The great war chief was amusing his guests with the tales of Captain Pierce's slaughter. They made a swift march in search of their prey.

Canonchet must have sensed some danger because he sent two of his men to the top of the hill above his camp. Seeing the English almost upon them, they turned and ran, leaving their leader to his fate. Another was sent out and ran at the sight. A fourth spy returned obediently to his master and reported the English upon them. Canonchet fled on foot, his Indian pursuers keeping tight pace with him. In the Blackstone River he fell and was laid hold of by a Pequot warrior. At last one of the leaders was in English hands. Forty prisoner were slain by the sword before Dennison set off for Stonington with his prize.

Canonchet was offered his life if he would become an ally of the English and fight for them. He refused. Though sentenced to death, he still defied his adversaries. To one writer who looked back later after these bitter days, he seemed the finest figure of any savage. The decision was made to allow all his enemies to share in his execution. He asked to be shot by Oneko who was equivalent in rank.

The Mohegans removed his head and quartered his body. The Ninnicrafts roasted it. In a gesture of love and fidelity, his head was sent to the Connecticut Council on April 8. So perished Canonchet, the most distinguished leader of men and a warrior of great renown. His death was a terrible loss to the Indian war effort.

Dennison later led a successful attack in which he killed or captured eighty and much seed corn. The capture of the seed corn was a greater loss to the Indians because it meant starvation. Dennison lost only one man killed. These two great victories were short-lived.

Through the support of the Narragansett, Philip was now the chief of the warring tribes. His emotion-driven hordes were ill-equipped and ill-organized. The war continued with Billerica, twenty-two miles northwest of Boston, attacked on April 9th, Chelmsford, six miles northwest of Billerica on the 15th.

Two days later the remains of Marlboro, twenty-seven miles south west of Chelmsford, was burned. On April 18th Weymouth, seventeen miles south of Boston, fell to the torch. On the 19th a soldier was killed in Hingham, four miles northeast of Weymouth and Bridgewater, sixteen miles south of Weymouth were attacked the same day. Wrentham, twenty-nine miles south of Weymouth, was raided later in the month - its deserted houses burned. Two houses containing smallpox sufferers were left untouched. From Casco Bay, one hundred and seven miles north of Boston to Stonington, fifty-three miles south of Providence, Rhode Island, smoke and flames consumed everything.

By the abandonment of Groton, Billerica, Lancaster and Marlboro, Sudbury, forty miles west of Boston, became the new target. On the banks of the Sudbury River it was a center for the roads that radiated out to the other settlements. Through its streets passed soldiers going to and from the valley finding shelter on their trip at the garrisons at Marlboro and Quabaug.

By the middle of April it had been attacked and a portion of the town burned. A relief force from Concord had been cut off and led into an ambush and slain or captured.

Captain Samuel Wadsworth was dispatched from Boston to relieve the garrison at Marlboro. He began his march without the full complement assigned to him, having only seventy-two volunteers. He moved through Sudbury which is ten miles nearer to Boston than Marlboro without detecting the five hundred braves led by Philip who lay waiting to strike Sudbury.

A small force of Indians had earlier in the day fired on the residents and burned a couple of houses, forcing them into the garrison. Believing this was the work of a small force, Wadsworth moved on to Marlboro which he reached about midnight.

At dawn on April 21st the force of Indians made a feint upon a poorly fortified garrison house until noon, the main garrison was unhurt.

Captain Edward Cowell with eighteen men marching from Quabaug to Boston, reached the town early in the morning. Abandoning the main road, he sought to approach the garrison in a circle, his men keeping the attackers at bay with numerous raising of their guns. He reached the garrison with the loss of only four men who had lagged behind and been cut off.

The news of the attack was soon known in Boston, Watertown and Concord. Eleven men sent from Concord, seven miles away, coming from the west were lured into an ambush in the river meadow, all but one being killed.

Captain Hugh Mason from Watertown, thirteen miles away, soon arrived on the opposite banks of the river, drove the attackers out of the village and crossed over the river to the west bank. He attempted to get to Green Hill where there was heavy firing but was driven back to the nearest garrison house. The firing at Green Hill grew fainter as the sun went down, leaving the hearers to worry and wonder at the defenders' fate.

Upon learning of the attack at Sudbury through which he had just recently passed, Captain Wadsworth retraced his steps back with was Captain Brockelbank and his fifty men who had been relieved. As he neared Green Hill, about a mile from Sudbury, a few warriors appeared among the trees. Though a veteran of the war, he did not realize the size of the force hiding around the town, supposing that they had already fled at his approach. As his men pursued the fleeing figures into the woods, they were suddenly fired on from all sides.

Fighting their way to the top of the hill, they held their own until night fall, loosing only five men during that four hour fight. The enemy set fire to the bushes and the soldiers fled through the smoke and the battle disintegrated into hand to hand combat.

One story relates an old Englishman who fled and was trapped in a swamp without a weapon. His captor mocked him with these word, "Come, Lord Jesus, save this poor Englishman whom I am about to kill." This was heard by another Englishman hiding in the bush close by. Our Patient, Long-suffering Lord permitted that bloody wretch (the Englishman) to knock him down and leave him dead."

Thirteen or fourteen Englishmen escaped to Noyes Mill, a quarter mile away.

On hearing the firing at Green Hill cease, Captain Mason assumed the offensive after having repulsed the Indians sent against him at the garrison. Knowing the mill's presence and that it was easily defensible, he surmised any survivors from the fight on Green Hill may have made their defense there.

Late that night they reached it without opposition, finding that the men had already been rescued by a force under Captain Samuel Hunting consisting of Indians scout and horsemen who had been dispatched there immediately on hearing of the fight.

Early the next morning Captain Mason found and buried the Concord men in the meadow. Only five were found, the others believed to have been taken prisoners and then tortured.

At Green Hill they gathered the naked bodies of Wadsworth, Brockelbank and twenty-seven others. They left the undiscovered bodies of those killed in the flight to the mill in the thicket. It was later learned that the few taken prisoners on Green Hill were, that night, forced to run the gauntlet and then tortured to death.

The Indians moved off to the west toward Marlboro where they were seen to fire seventy-four volleys into the air for the lives they had taken at Sudbury. They then fired the remaining houses at Marlboro and stole the cattle. In this attack they had been overly bold, Sudbury only about twenty miles from Boston.

Captain Hunting's force of friendly Indians appearing here was of great significance. The Boston Council had finally yielded to the requests of Eliot, the preacher who had amassed the Praying Indians, and their officers in the field, Gookin, Savage, Henchman and Prentice, to trust the friendly Indians. They had finally forsook their ramrod Puritan ethics to realize the necessities of Indian warfare.

The disasters of constant ambushes and losses were in the past and the knowledge of how to fight like an Indian soon led to the collapse of their opponents.

Scituate, thirty miles south of Boston, was attacked the same day, but the warriors were beaten off and only burned a few houses and barns. These were the last big victories that the warring Indians were to realize in the remaining length of hostilities. The forces amassed against them would soon turn the war's favor to the Englishmen.

It was obvious the war was taking a greater toll on the Indians. With Canonchet gone, his plan to raise food was abandoned and jealous quarrels kept them separated and isolated. The English now fought in the same manner, parties roaming the countryside, burning villages and fields. The hostiles faced starvation and disease was everywhere rampant. Their excesses and elation of spirit had turned to depression.

Small bands begun to appear and surrender while others parleyed for the release of white and friendly

Indian captives. Giving up captives was vehement-
ly opposed by the Narragansett. Many a hard fight
would soon follow and many Englishman bite the
dust, but the tide of the Indian war had begun to
wane.

On May 5th, 1676 near Mendon, Massachusetts,
fifty miles south of Boston, a Natick scouting party under Captain Henchman from Connecticut surprised a large hunting party and killed several. Returning to their camp at Medfield, that night they
saw two hundred campfires in the vicinity.

Harassed by colds and disease Henchman had to
disband his soldiers by the 10th without any further
results.

On May 8th Bridgewater was attacked again, the
settlers able to drive the warriors off but not before
they burned thirteen houses. On May 11th they
assaulted Halifax, a suburb thirteen miles west of
Plymouth, destroying eleven houses and five barns,
the residents having fled to a safe garrison.

The Indians returned a few days later and fin-
ished burning seven more houses and two more
barns and completed the destruction of Middleboro,
fifteen miles east of Plymouth, and then Nemasket,
3 miles further west.

On May 12th after a force of warriors had driven
off over seventy head of livestock the settlers had
gathered to pasture, the irate men in the garrison
at Hatfield could stand no more. As they gathered
to strike, Thomas Read who had been a captive

with Mrs. Rowlandson camp into town and told of the location of a large fishing village of over seven hundred men, women and children and about seventy warriors on the Connecticut River at Turner's Falls.

On May 18th Captain William Turner and Captain Samuel Holyoke left Hatfield with one hundred and eighty mounted men to strike at their foe.

Turner, a Baptist, had originally been denied a commission because of his religion, but the dire needs of Massachusetts won over their prejudices again and he was given a command. Samuel Holyoke was the grandson of William Pynchon, the founder of Springfield, Massachusetts.

After a tiring eighteen mile march, the force surprised the sleeping Indians, they had not even bothered to post sentries.

Unfortunately Captain Holyoke set the tone for a massacre when he discovered five or six old men, women and children cowering under a rock ledge.

The same fate was dealt out to women and children and warriors alike. Without hesitation he slew them with his sword. Divine justice for those who shed innocent blood cannot be ignored, however.

Holyoke, the 29 year-old slayer of the innocent, soon died from the rigors of this campaign.

Many warriors escaped leaving the women and children behind to be their death. One hundred were killed or drowned attempting to escape in the river. The English destroyed their ammunition and their provisions, an even greater loss than the men. But the attackers paid for their success as a fierce counter-attack from the other two nearby villages was mounted after the Indians ascertained the numbers against them. The soldiers panicked and separated to try and escape. Only by Captain Holyoke's efforts did most revive and so save their lives.

After the savage fighting Captain Turner lay dead along with thirty eight of his men, a stinging blow to an otherwise successful campaign.

This was the last full scale battle against a united Indian foe. After this the engagements became sporadic and unplanned. The sudden collapse of the Indian resistance was surprising to the English who were at their wits end to conclude the war.

Poorly armed and equipped throughout the war, the Indian resistance succumbed to attrition of hunger, battle losses and disease. The palisaded and garrisoned towns no longer afforded them the free supplies they needed to continue. And the English use of Indian tactics against them took its toll.

On May 20th, not ready to give up, the Indians hit Scituate a second time and burned the mill and then were driven off. Because of the inclement weather, the muddy roads and the sickness of the men, the English for the most part stayed in garrison in hopes of the peace talks coming to fruition. Only in the southeast between Providence and Medfield had forces been dispatched.

On May 30th the Indians struck at Hatfield, burning

twelve houses and barns and gathering many sheep for their food. At Hadley just across the river, the townspeople gathered a force of 25 who crossed the river and charged them in their feast. The Indians outnumbered them ten to one but let them past after the soldiers' first volley killed five or six.

Five of the rescuers were killed as they reached the town. The Indians withdrew leaving behind twenty-five bodies.

By the end of May, encouraged by the need to end the war before the whole country was destroyed and no longer overly concerned about the captives who might fall under the tomahawk, the authorities worked tirelessly to bring together men, weapons and clothing that so many needed.

Captain Benjamin Newberry, commander of the military department for Connecticut, was second-in-command to Major Talcott. With eighty men he took up vigil at Northampton. He fought three hundred Indians at Quabaug and was then ordered to march to Hadley.

On June 8th Major John Talcott from Norwich had arrived with two hundred and fifty whites and two hundred Mohegans.

On the night of June 11th a band of seven hundred Indians crept upon Hadley. In the meantime Captain Benjamin Henchman with his 500 foot and horse and friendly Indians had left Concord to meet up with Talcott at Quabaug. The Indians were busy watching his slow progress and had missed the arrival of Talcott at Hadley.

Unaware of the large force awaiting within, they attacked on the night of June 11th. The band was driven away from the town and pursued several miles by the English forces, no longer to come upon the reinforced center of the English army. Henchman arrived on the 14th and two days later the combined forces started a sweep up the Connecticut River. Sadly, at Turner's Falls they found the bodies of Captain Turner and his men and buried them.

The summer brought more lonely settlers who had refused to leave their farms under the enemy's gun, but the towns were now relatively safe. There were no longer large bands of Indians on the prowl and forces sent out under experienced captains to locate them kept the warriors and their dependents on the run, leaving them no time to attack. They could no longer encamp for more than a day or two before they must again scatter.

On June 20th Talcott was recalled to Connecticut and Henchman back to Boston. Henchman received word that Philip had returned to Mount Hope and the Boston authorities ordered forces under Moseley back out to meet up with Woodcock's garrison and to follow an Indian guide to Philip's camp. By the time he reached there with his seventy-six men, their prey had flown the trap. In the meantime, there was still plenty of opportunity for the enemy to strike unsuspecting farmers which they did.

June 21st was set aside as a day of humiliation and prayer and the 29th as a day of thanksgiving by colonist who were sending supplies and men to keep the Indians on the run.

On July 1st while lurking on the outskirts of Swansea, a small band of Philip's followers killed a farmer, Hezekiah Willet, carrying away his head as a trophy along with his Negro servant.

The end of June Major Talcott returned to start his next campaign. On July 2nd his force fell upon a Narragansett camp in a swamp on the south bank of the Pawtuxet River near Natick, seven miles from Providence. The mounted Englishmen closed in on all sides of the swamp while the Mohegans and Pequot rushed down the hill toward the camp. Forty-five women and children were captured and one hundred twenty-six, including thirty-four warriors, slain with the sword and tomahawk. Only one friendly Indian was killed and the whole affair was deemed indiscriminate massacre of the helpless.

Talcott then marched to Providence and thence in a sweep through the neck, killing and capturing sixty-seven more Indians. Running low on supplies, he turned to go back to Providence.

During this march one of the prisoners who had taunted the friendly Indians he allowed to be tortured to death by the Mohegans in a most terrible manner. Though reluctant to allow it, the English desired to appease their Indian allies and at the same time had a curiosity to see such a spectacle.

They got much more than they had bargained for. The Revered William Hubbard, who witnessed this affair, judged it an act "to remind us to bless the Father of Lights who has called us out of the dark places of the earth."

Talcott was condemned for not stopping this savage treatment which he lent approval to by being present. To the Mohegans it was normal practice but the English who could not bear the cruelty watched with tears in their eyes. On July 11th Philip attempted to attack Taunton but the settlement was warned by Willet's Negro who had escaped his captors.

On July 14th Bridgewater was attacked yet again, but being filled with young men who had refused to give up their farms, the attack was beaten back. The Connecticut force left behind by Talcott captured seventy-five Indians in two forays.

The Boston Council now offered the hostile Indians an opportunity to surrender within 14 days and receive mercy. By July 6, three hundred Plymouth and Cape Code Indians along with their sachems had accepted the offer. Sagamore Sam, a Nashaway, who had helped redeem many English captives, wrote the Council in hopes of mercy for him and other sachems. When no word was sent to them, they fled in terror to the northern frontier of Maine. The English were not ready to extend mercy to the chiefs who had participated in this war. Some sachems fought to the end, one being Pumham who was surprised near Dedham, just ten miles south of Boston, by Captain Hunting. In the fight he was shot in the back and fought to the death with his tomahawk. Fifteen were killed and 34 captured.

On July 22nd the Massachusetts force returned to Boston, some to be disbanded, others to be sent to New Hampshire and Maine where the war on the eastern frontier was raging. Their services were no longer required in Massachusetts where the Nipmucks had given up.

Fugitive bands continued to give up and sometimes bring with them sachems whom the English considered "murderous."

All who had been involved in the murder of a colonist or the destruction of property were executed. Hundreds were shipped to the West Indies, Spain, Portugal, Bermuda and Virginia.

Plymouth alone sold five hundred into slavery. Rhode Island under Roger Williams refused to participate in such barbarous treatment, limiting their sale of prisoners to limited indentured servitude within their colony. Some who surrendered were given land to settle on and young children, especially in Connecticut, were settled amongst the settlers as apprentices.

Uncas, who had fought with the whites, found his tribe shunned when the Court in Hartford ruled that the English had won the war and the Mohegans would receive no pay in prisoners. His people had to submit in humility to the meager rewards which were far less than they had earned. In a few generations they shrank down to a meager remnant just as had their old enemy, the Narragansett.

Pursued by the whites and friendly Indians, the plight of the hostile Indian tribes was extreme to the point of being exterminated. With the departure of the Massachusetts troops, stamping out the remaining resistance fell to the Plymouth colony forces of Major Bradford and Captain Church. Bradford chose a defensive plan of holding the fords on the Taunton River and covering the town. Not so Church. He was ready to go on the attack.

While the Connecticut River campaigns were underway, Plymouth colony feared for its survival after hearing of the attack on Lancaster.

Having recovered from his wounds received at the Great Swamp Fight, on the 25th of February, Captain Church was asked to command a mere sixty or seventy men. He refused saying he must have at least 200 to be able to hold his own. The Plymouth council continued to quibble about the debt they were incurring and refused his request to raise volunteers and friendly Indians.

In disgust in the early part of March he decided to move his family who lived at the supposedly safe garrison at Clark's Island near Plymouth over the protestations of her wife's parents.

Within 24 hours of their arrival in Rhode Island, the Clark's Island garrison was overrun and all killed as has been described formerly. This God's hand to save a man who would save the colony.

By the early part of June after the birth of his second son, Church was given the go-ahead. Plymouth would send out two hundred men to which Boston and Connecticut would add additional troops. He was ordered to return to Rhode Island to recruit from the many families who had fled there for refuge. While returning from Plymouth to Narragansett Bay on this canoe trip, he came upon some Saconet Indians whom he knew and conferred with them, suspecting that they were hardly tired of the war. He agreed to come back in two days time for a parley with Queen Awashonks, his old friend.

On reaching Rhode Island he asked permission of his military seniors to carry out this liaison. They feared it was a trick and at first refused. When he persisted in his reasoning they allowed him to go without their blessings. Next he had to convenience his wife who was beside herself with fear for his safety. She finally assented and the next morning he set out with two canoes. In one was he and his own man and in the other the two Indians who had paddled him up the river.

At the appointed meeting place he found the queen with her chief men. As they walked together to a comfortable meeting place, they were immediately surrounded by armed and ferocious warriors.

Undaunted by this unplanned turn of events, Church demanded they lay down their guns if they were truly wanting to talk peace. This they did then returned to the council. After Church had passed around a bottle of rum and tobacco for all present, he turned to his hostess and waited for her to speak.

Awashonks explained to Church that if he had come to aid her when she made the original treaty of peace, she would never have joined Philip. He lamented that in his attempt to come to her aid with nineteen men, they had been set upon and had a fierce fight all afternoon. One among the group, Little Eyes, raised his tomahawk to revenge his brother who had led the party against Church and been killed. The captain chief now demanded silence so that the talk should return to the present and not old wounds.

The Saconets agreed they would submit and serve the whites if they could be guaranteed not to be sold into slavery. The chief captain vowed they would fight with the whites to secure Philip's head.

With this promise Church returned to his wife in Rhode Island. Awashonks at once called in her warriors and marched to meet the assembling English army at Pocasset under the command of Major Bradford. Church had to defy Bradford's refusal to use the Indians and set out for Plymouth to secure permission which was given. They offered him a large contingent of English men which he refused, preferring to take, instead, only half a dozen with him and some horses he picked up at Sandwich.

Along the coast they found a large assembly of Indians, all sexes and ages, involved in a sporting contest. Finding them to be Awashonks' people he was invited to join them. He and his men watched as all the warriors present went through a swearing ceremony, dancing before a huge bonfire and showing their prowess in fighting the hostile tribes as they were named by the chief captain in his dance.

Little Eyes, the murderous warrior, invited Church to step aside with him (at which time he would have attempted to slay the captain). Church, the ever wise Indian fighter, declined the invitation. Awashonk now informed him that he could call on any of these warriors as he needed them. To finalize the agreement she presented him with a mighty fine musket.

Selecting several fighting men he set out the next day for Plymouth where he was joined by a small group of Englishmen. Not waiting for rest, he led his force straightaway into the forest in search of the Narragansett.

Stealing into the July corn fields, they captured a whole group of Narragansetts, not one escaping. Taking them to Plymouth they were all sold into slavery. That was the agreement Church had with the Plymouth authorities. Plymouth would take half the prisoners and the soldiers the other half, the Indians to take all plunder and arms.

These expeditions became no more than sanctioned slave-hunts.

For the next three weeks with his bodyguard Jeffrey, a captured Narragansett, Church never came back empty- handed. Capturing one or two lone Indians at a time, he forced them to reveal the presence of their camps. Plymouth now saw the positive results of employing the friendly Indians and had to admit Church was both brave and discreet. So the contract was amended. He was ordered to raise a company of two hundred men, including Indians as long as the English numbered sixty of the total.

He was allowed free range of not only Plymouth but the whole Confederation. So in the period of a short two months, from May when the authorities were out of ideas and the Indians were attacking with impunity, the tide of hopes for the colonist had turned on this brave man. It further allowed him "to discover, pursue, destroy, fight, surprise or subdue our Indian enemies . . . by treaty and composition to receive mercy (provided they not be Murderous Rogues or such as have been principal actors in those Villanies. . . Faithfully to serve the Interests of God, his Majesty's Interest and the Interest of the Colony." With this contract he became the most active commander left in the field.

This commission gave Church great power and authority. One such expedition involved escorting a train of supplies carts to Major Bradford at Taunton. Creeping forward to Middleboro he surprised and captured eighteen Indians and on reaching Taunton turned them over to the major and went 'a hunting.'

Learning from the prisoners of the location of a large body of Indians, he immediately pursued during the night pushing his men to their endurance until they must stop and camp in a grassy valley.

Guards were posted at the Cushnet River, north of New Bedford, and sentinels around the camp; then all fell asleep including the guards - God in his Providence protected their slumber and before dawn they were able to creep upon the a small camp. To his amazement it was the same Little Eyes who had challenged him in Awashonks' camp and then left in opposition to his Queen. Instead of attacking, Church offered him his life which he accepted. Little did he know of the slavery that would follow because of his murderous past. Leaving the prisoners to be guarded on an island in the river by friendly Indians led by Lightfoot, the army pushed forward until night fell and rested again at North Dartmouth, a deserted town three miles west of New Bedford, Connecticut.

Following a trail out of town, Church found it soon forked. The Indian guides were told this was their opportunity to redeem themselves, as he would allow them to go along one fork and his men another, later to meet at a designated location. His Indian guides had advised that he split his men so as to make a lesser target of one larger body. At the same time Major Bradford was beating up the country with his larger force and any Indians he came against would run in fear, thinking it the larger army.

Finding a large group of Indians picking berries, he and his bodyguard on the finest horses, rode in amongst them shouting to them surrender. Most took to flight and in pursuit, Church and his single interpreter were soon out of sight of their men.

They continued to round up prisoners and drive them back to his men, capturing or killing sixty-six Indians in this mad pursuit. The prisoners informed him there was a large camp in the swamps with one hundred warriors gone on a hunt for provisions at the settlers' expense.

Their scouts discovered the warriors returning, each man carrying his load of meat, but did not reveal their presence so that the army could get past them undetected.

Picking up Little Eyes and his group, they pushed on to the rendezvous. There it was found each party had identical results, sixty-three prisoners and three killed by each group.

However, the Indians had come upon a town inhabited by one of Philip's chiefs. On seeing the shouting and firing Saconets the warriors had fled in panic leaving behind their women and children and their guns. Among the prisoners was Philip's wife and son who were later sold into slavery in the West Indies and so disappeared the great clan of Massosoit who had been 40 years a true friend to the Plymouth colony. A large force could have captured the whole town.

Unknown to Church, Philip lay in ambush along the road to Plymouth. Church, an experienced warrior himself, never took the same road going as coming and so out-foxed the fox.

On August 6th, Wetamoo, the wife of Quinnopan, who had so mistreated Mrs. Rowlandson met a fate that only God could have designed. Attempting to flee with her clan, most of whom were captured, she sought to cross the Taunton River on a log and due to exhaustion or hunger, was drowned. Her body was found along the river and her head cut off and displayed in Taunton. Her people who recognized the grisly remains cried out at the sight. Mrs. Rowlandson had her own opinion on her former mistresses' fate, "A severe dame she was, bestowing every day in dressing herself near as much time as any gentry in the land: powdering her hair and painting her face, going with her necklaces, with jewels in her ears and bracelets upon her arms."

Another author says that such treatment meted out to the dead body of a white women would have sent the Reverend Cotton Mather seeking God's word on the barbaric act.

Church was a natural reader of the human soul. Amongst his prisoners he would pick out those he fancied and offer them mercy if they fought beside him. Those that responded with contempt he would slap on the back and say that it was of no consequence. Most lost their surliness and soon took arms against their own kin.

Philip, on the other hand, faced dark days. Major Bradford, a Connecticut force under Major Talcott, and Church were hot on his heels. On July 30 a message came to Governor Winslow at Marshfield that a strong force of the enemy was about to hit either Bridgewater or Taunton. Hurrying to Plymouth he called out all the men even though it was the middle of morning services as the enemy was want to attack during that time. Church, who was summoned from the meeting house, assembled his men and the newly enlisted volunteers who poured out of the church.

Philip, finding the area too dangerous for his men, was headed back to the Nipmuck country to the south. Hewing down a tree to cross the Taunton River, he led his party across.

A scouting party of English from Bridgewater which is north of Taunton found the ford and fired upon the party crossing at the time, killing Philip's old uncle and several men with him.

When Church came to the area the next day he was about to fire on an Indian sitting in the middle but hesitated when his guide said it may be a friend. As he held his fire, he saw that it was Philip himself.

Even though they waded across rivers up to their armpits, the Plymouth men could not close the gap between them and their fleeing enemy. A rest was called. The Indian force with him kept on and next morning brought in thirteen more prisoners.

Pressing on in the chase, Church finally caught up to the main body which had stopped to camp for the night. He rested his men during the night close to the enemy. The next morning, he instructed the prisoners that he could not leave a guard and that they must not attempt to escape since he had captured hundreds of their number, that they should follow his track since to try to escape was useless.

Again, Church's shrewdness paid off. Not a prisoner was lost. Two of Church's' advance guard were sent out to find the camp and met two of Philip's scout who fled to their camp, howling and screaming.

Church charged the camp but found only half-cooked breakfast. The pursued had disappeared into the swamp. He then split his force, each body moving around the swamp to meet at the other side. To their surprise, the fleeing Wampanoags faced the muskets of the English as they emerged from their brier patch.

Shouting at them to surrender or all would be killed gave his men time to close in and snatch loaded and cocked weapons before they could be discharged.

Moving the large number of prisoners to a nearby valley, he left them under guard and continued his pursuit.

Those Indians who had escaped from the camp

had rallied to creep upon Church's flank. A quick volley into their midst sent them running again. In this swamp fight, Church and two men who always stayed as his bodyguards met three Indians. Two surrendered, but the third, being a burly warrior with two locks tied up with red and a great rattlesnake skin hanging from his head, escaped into the swamp. Away went Church who caught the fellow and fired, but the damp of the fog had spoiled his powder. The Indian turned and attempted to fire with the same result. Turning for another run, he tripped over a root and went down on his face. Church dispatched him with a pistol shot to the back of the head.

Looking behind him, Church saw a man he thought had been killed, charging down upon him. Within gun shot range of the guards around the two prisoners, they brought down the man though not without a near miss to their captain's person.

One hundred and seventy-three Indians had been captured or killed in this swamp raid including the prisoners they had taken the day before who had obeyed Church's instructions.

A messenger was sent to Bridgewater to instruct them to prepare for the arrival of the force with the prisoners and the need for provisions. That night, the prisoners in the pound, shouted and laughed with the townspeople after a good feeding.

The prisoners told Church that Philip would be ready to die after this blow to his people.

Several minor expeditions followed until in August King Philip was captured.

On August 11th Church, being at Pocasset, rhode Island with his force, endeavored to visit his wife who was only eight miles away. His home-coming was cut short when two riders appeared, Major Sanford and Captain Roger Golding, the same man who had sailed his sloop down the river to rescue Church and his men the previous year.

They came in great haste to report Philip was at Mount Hope as reported by a deserter whose brother Philip had just slain over some offense. The deserter described the camp's exact location. Church, well familiar with the terrain, sped to the chase and approached during the night.

On the morning of August 14th He gave Captain Golding instructions on how to approach the camp and survey it without sounding an alarm. As soon as they were discovered, they should cry out and drive the Indians into the swamp where Church would have an ambush waiting.

He positioned an Indian and a soldier together behind trees around the swamp with instructions to fire at any who would try to escape.

Golding in his anxiousness, thought an Indian had spied him and ordered his men to fire into the sleeping camp, thus missing them and firing over their head. The majority of the fleeing Indians were soon in the swamp.

Philip in the lead with only a small breech cloth

and stockings, and his gun ran immediately into two of Church's men, Caleb Cook and an Indian companion. The Englishman's gun misfired, but the Indian's shot took Philip in the heart and another two inches from it. The great chief fell face down in the swamp on top of his gun.

Philip's captain, Annawan, tried to rally his men during the fight, but they were concerned only with escape. Finding an unguarded point, they ran through it leaving their chief in the mud and water.

Philip's body was dragged out of the swamp and since he had left many an Englishman unburied, Church ordered part of his body to be left so. An Indian was ordered to cut off the head and quarter the body as befits a rebel under English law. The Indian declared as he raised his tomahawk that this big man who had made so many men fall would soon come to an end.

The head went to Plymouth arriving there on August 17th which had been proclaimed a day of solemn thanksgiving. It was displayed on a pole for more than 20 years until about 1700. The hands went to Boston and the quartered body hung in four tree above where he had fallen.

This being a Saturday, Church and his force crossed over into Rhode Island and the following Tuesday went to Plymouth to receive their pay, thirty schillings per person killed or captured, including Philip's head.

Philip's story was written by his enemies. Remember the old saying - history is recorded by the victor. More current readers safely removed from the theological and racial opinions of this war can judge the cause of Philip's rebellion. His resentment against the English and his Indian pride drug him into a season of mistrust and hate of the tyranny of his white neighbors.

He was, owing to circumstances, forced into the limelight as the first sachem to break the peace. His attempts as a statesman in winning over the other tribes in an inevitable war cannot be denied.

As chief, if he felt that war with the whites was the only way to save his people, then he had to form such alliances to insure his success. As a warrior he was surpassed by Canonchet. His outstanding traits were the ability to foresee the needs of his confederation and act as the organizer behind the scenes.

His failure was his inability to win all the tribes and hold back his young bucks until a full-scale attack could be launched. Charges of cruelty were never substantiated whereas he made an effort to save Mrs. Rowlandson and other families he considered his friends. To the Indians he was a patriot.

Some writers have offered the eulogy that he fought to the end against his fate and against an enemy that, due to its higher civilized nature, deserved to win. The circumstances leading to the war and its conduct were abhorrent. The two races were so at odds that conflict was inevitable and the harsh measures of the colonists in this struggle were necessary.

Four days after Philip was killed, Quinnopan was captured, tried at Newport and shot the next day along with his brother.

In a single year of fighting, so savage had the war been, that the colonists had become as brutal as their enemies. So it was with widespread joy that the people celebrated the end of their great arch enemy.

Many ministers rose up in the pulpits and declared that "So let all thine enemies perish, Lord." All this fiery rhetoric did was arouse the rabble of Boston who wanted to go at once to Deer Island and slay all the Praying Indians who had taken refuge there. The educated men of the colonies, the mayors, magistrates, ministers and officers should have countered this nonsense, but few did.

Though the Indian forces had begun to disperse, there were renegades requiring Church to hunt them down. His next target was Annawan, Philip's chief captain, who had escaped the Mount Hope swamp and was reported to be near Rehoboth.

On August 28th his men set out to capture the chief who was hiding now in a swamp a few miles north of Mattapoiset, located east of New Bedford. The compensation was so small that Church could raise only half a dozen men plus his faithful friend, Jabez Howland, and a few friendly Indians.

On crossing from Prudence Is- land to Poppasquash Neck, the force was split up due to bad weather with only his Indians across. They assented to go alone with the Englishmen left behind.

The loyal Lightfoot who had been the guard to many a captured prisoner was sent with his companions to spy out the area. With him was a recently captured Indian, Nathanael, who knew the current sounds the Indians were using to communicate. By the hoot of an owl or the howling of a wolf the natives communicated with one another in the forest. These calls were changed any time it was thought the whites would have found out the code.

In such a manner, two hunters were captured who were found skinning a horse. These two reported a party of eighteen hunters were out and would rendezvous there shortly. In like manner all eighteen were captured.

Nathanael spoke so well of his new captain that they were all converted over to join their force. By then Jabez Howland and his men had appeared.

That night, friendly Indian, converted Indian and white men ate well on horse meat. The next morning the force was led to where the hunters' families awaited fresh meat and they were added to the force. One captive asked to go after his old father who was living with his squaw in a swamp.

Taking one white man and several Indians with him, Church set out to seek Annawan. On reaching the swamp, the young savage began to make the wolf howl seeking out his father.

Capture of an old man and his squaw resulted in him telling  of the main camp. The old man swore he would protect Church from all attackers but refused to take up a musket against his old master.

With only one Englishman and several Indians, Church had to decide whether to go up against fifty warriors. If he waited for the main body, time would be lost. He asked the Englishman if he dared go. He replied he was never afraid to go anywhere with Church. The Indians agreed.

Church was directed to the main camp of fifty or sixty which he reached at sunset. It was located at the bottom of a steep and rocky ledge, inaccessible from any other direction. Quietly he followed the old man and squaw into camp, surprising the occupants who surrendered without resistance.

Annawan rose up and after a startled cry offered them welcome. During the night his exhausted troops slept among their captives who made no effort to escape.

As Church watched, the old chief, after pacing back and forth before the fire, disappeared and then returned and bowed before him offering up Philip's royal robes, two belts of wampum for the waist and head, a red cloth blanket and two horns of powder, saying, "You have killed Philip and captured his country, for I believe that I and my company are the last to war against the English, so I suppose the war is ended by your means; these things belong to you." Church in return promised him his life (even if it was to be sold as a slave). The two captains sat together before the fire all night, exchanging tales of combat.

Going back to his peaceful farming, Church had only a short respite before he was called in September to go after another outlaw - Philip's brother-in-law, Tuspaquin whose camp was found after his followers had spent much time making trouble in the area of Lippican, killing the settlers' livestock.

The main fugitive camp was discovered much like Annawan, the unsuspecting sitting around their campfires. Tuspaquin's wife and son were captured, but he was told the sachem was gone to kill horses, which the Indians looked on as a delicacy. Church wanted to enlist this great warrior in the war that was now raging fierce on the eastern frontier. He left two old squaws to deliver the message that Tuspaquin's life and that of his family would be spared if he became Church's soldier. The unfortunate sachem who came to Plymouth when Church was absent did not receive the promised leniency.

Church, on his return, found that the court had over-turned his promises and both Tuspaquin and Annawan had been executed, over-ruling Church's authority and his pledge for their lives. Church, with only 20 men and their Indian allies, had captured or killed 700 in two months.

While forces were scouring other areas, Connecticut was unguarded. Through this perimeter many bands of Indians escaped to the west in the area of the Hudson River. Major Talcott followed a large band on August 11th which had crossed the Chicopee River and passed near Westfield, fourteen miles south of Hartford, Connecticut.

On the 15th he overtook them at the Housatonic River in camp. Attempting to surround them in the night, a lone fisherman gave the surprise of their presence and paid with his life. Talcott killed thirty-five and captured twenty, some two hundred escaping to the Hudson where they were received and incorporated into the Mohawks.

The Indians who had fled to New York caused much worry and concern. Governor Andros refused to allow authorities to pursue the fugitives into his state. He also refused to turn over any in his jurisdiction.

Meanwhile, Captain Swain by orders from Boston collected men from the garrisons at Hadley, Hatfield, and Northampton and marched to destroy the growing corn crops at Deerfield and Northampton. Thus ended the conflict in the areas that Philip had waged war, though the struggle continued well into the next year in the north and east.

Starving bands of vagrants continued to haunt the woods, hunted down by the friendly Indians. In December a band of sixty was captured near Rehoboth.

Before turning to the war in the north and east, a summary of the damage done to Massachusetts, Rhode Island and Plymouth must be examined.

Two-thirds of all the towns and settlements in these areas had been attacked with a dozen utterly destroyed. 8-10% (600) of all men in the colonies able to bear arms (some 6,000) had been killed or were missing in battle, presumably captured and tortured to death at the hands of their captors.

This was augmented by the hundreds of old men, women and children who were slain in their homes, front yards and fields. Over six hundred dwellings fell to the Indian's torch along with thousands of head of livestock and a year's harvest. But crops survived and hunger did not threaten the survivors.

This short fierce war had been waged without help from England. The four colonies paid dearly in material goods as well. The debt to Plymouth of one hundred thousand pounds sterling exceeded all personal wealth of its inhabitants which the people immediately set to work to repay.

The Indians had been virtually exterminated, the land transferred to the victors. The estimates of their loses is three thousand killed and many times that wounded or captured.

Only a few scattered villages remained of the Narragansett. The valley Indians were never seen again except for one raid a year later when they came out of hiding in Canada and attacked Hatfield and Deerfield, killing several and carrying away 24 captives, most of whom were later ransomed.

# Sioux Uprising of 1862

In August of 1862, the U.S. government was three months late in delivering the year's annuity payment of $71,000 to the Santee Sioux. By treaty, the Sioux had been forced into a narrow stretch of land on the south banks of the Minnesota River.

The traders at the agencies, whose warehouses were full of food and trade goods, had no faith that the government payment would come through because of the fact that the Civil War was raging at the time. Meanwhile, the Indians were starving.

Some Indians went to the Northern Agency to ask for a credit extension prepared for conflict. A deal was made and further credit was extended.

When another group of Indians went to the Southern Agency, the trader there by the name of Myrick - even though he was married to a Sioux woman, said, "Let them eat grass."

To tell the story of what happened next we have taken an excerpt from our book - _Fire Hair_.

Near a place called Acton, Minnesota, four young men of the Dakotah or Santee Sioux Indian Nation sat around a fire in their small camp. They were hungry, very hungry, angry and emotionally drained.

The braves were part of Chief Shakopee's band from the north side of the Minnesota River. This chief had approximately forty men of the warrior age in his band. The names of these young men were Brown Wing, Breaking Up, Killing Ghost and Runs Against Something When Crawling.

Killing Ghost said, "We have traveled over a hundred miles looking for game and have found none." "It's the white man's fault we have nothing to eat," said Runs Against Something When Crawling.

"The white man comes and cuts our land with his plow. He kills our game. What does he leave us to eat?" asked Brown Wing as he tossed a willow branch he had been chewing into the fire.

"This is not our land anymore," complained Breaking Up. "Our chiefs gave our land away by treaty. The treaty they made years ago has our people in a strip of land that is twenty-two miles wide and seventy miles long on the north side of the Minnesota River. We are fortunate they allow us to roam free over this country to hunt and gather."

"You call this hunting and gathering?" Ghost Killer asked in a harsh tone, his face full of anger. "The white man has killed or scared off all the game in this entire country. He hunts so that there is nothing left for us to gather. He has everything and we have nothing."

Breaking Up took a conciliatory tone to calm his friends. "Chief Shakopee has said there shall be money coming to the agencies soon and we will all get our allotments and have full bellies again."

"He said that two months ago," said Runs Against Something When Crawling. "The whites now fight among themselves and they have taken our money to pay for their fight."

Ghost Killer stood up. "Yes, their Civil War has taken our money."

Breaking Up raised his hand. "But, the Upper Agency has been issuing credit so the children do not starve."

"The Upper Agency is run by a man who cares," said Ghost Killer. "Myrick, the trader at the Lower Agency, on the Redwood River is bad, even if he has an Indian wife. He said he would not give credit to the people and 'If they are hungry, they can eat grass.'"

Breaking Up raised his hand a second time. "We are all hungry and you are very angry, but Chief Shakopee has said the allotment money will be here before the new moon. We must sleep now and go into the big woods tomorrow and hunt."

The next day was Sunday, August 17. The hunting party turned out at first light and began to follow the trail north toward the big woods. The trail they were on soon crossed a white man's road. The road pointed north in a very straight line so they turned and followed it.

As they followed the road, they soon came to a section of fence around a corn field. They could see two cabins about a quarter of a mile away on their right.

Runs Against Something When Crawling was walking his horse at the head of the group when he suddenly slid from his mount and ran to the fence. He pulled three eggs from a nest and held them high for his companions to see. "Food. I have found food!" he exclaimed.

"Don't take them," said Breaking Up. "We could get into trouble."

"Put them back," said Ghost Killer. "You don't want to make the white man angry."

Runs Against Something When Crawling became very angry and dashed the eggs to the ground causing them to splatter on the road. "Cowards! You are all cowards. You won't even take an egg when you are half starved."

Ghost Killer dismounted to stand in front of his agitated companion. His eyes were open wide at the unexpected actions of his friend.

Runs Against Something When Crawling placed his finger on the chest of Ghost Killer. "You! You are the biggest coward of all, and when we get home, I am going to tell everyone what a coward you are."

Ghost Killer could not turn away from the challenge. "I am not a coward. I am not afraid of the white man, and to show you that I am not, I will go to the house and shoot him. Are you brave enough to go with me?"

Runs Against Something When Crawling turned his head up to the braves still on their ponies. "Yes, I will go with you, and we will see who is the braver."

Breaking Up looked over at Brown Wing and then

back at Runs Against Something When Crawling. "We will go with you, and we will be brave, too."

When the farmer, Robinson Jones saw the band of Indians galloping up his driveway he threw down the axe he was using to cut wood and ran next door to the house of his son-in-law, Howard Baker where there were other white visitors.

In the house, finishing breakfast, was Baker, Mr. Webster, Mrs. Jones and a fourteen year old girl. All of the occupants came out of the house and stood on the front porch, the girl, half hidden by the porch roof support post. Mr. Webster and Mr. Baker carried caplock muzzle loading rifles.

"What is it, you want?" Mr. Jones asked.

"We are hunting," said Ghost Killer. He eyed the armed men. "You have fine hunting weapons." He slid from his horse, handing the reins and his rifle to Brown Wing. He walked to the porch. "Can I see that fine gun of yours?" he asked Mr. Baker.

Hesitating, Baker stood a little straighter while looking over at Mr. and Mrs. Jones, both of whom shrugged their shoulders and tipped their heads in the affirmative.

Baker handed the gun to Ghost Killer who held it side-ways in front of himself for a moment running his hand over the barrel and the stock.

"A very nice hunting gun," he said, cocking the hammer and firing the ball into Baker at point blank range.

As if the first shot was a signal, the other braves

raised their guns and fired at the remaining people on the porch.

All but the girl dropped dead where they stood. She sprang from the porch and ran toward the barn. Ghost Killer picked up the gun of Mr. Webster and shot her in the back. She fell forward and rolled twice stopping just short of the barn door.

Brown Wing slid from his horse and pulled his knife as he approached the porch and the body of Jones.

Ghost Killer reached out his arm to pull Baker's body toward him. "They shall know they were killed by the Sioux. I will scalp this one and cut slashes in his feet so he can not walk in the Happy Hunting Ground, then all will know it was the People that killed him."

After scalping and hacking off Jones's hands, Brown Wing went into the house and was now back in the doorway waving a loaf of bread over his head. "They have more food than I have ever seen!" he exclaimed.

Runs Against Something When Crawling who had been at the barn dismembering the girl's body rushed into the house. There on the table were the dirty breakfast dishes, food still on some. Platters of meat, potatoes and eggs sat unattended. Cramming the leftovers into his face, he spoke through a food-filled mouth, "We shall celebrate this victory."

When all the braves had eaten their fill, Ghost Killer found two pipes and a canister of tobacco on the mantle. They sat back, relaxed and shared a smoke.

"Brown Wing and Breaking Up," said Ghost Killer, now the obvious leader, "go to the barn and hitch up a team to a wagon. We will take what we can to our village."

Breaking Up thumped his chest. "We have killed them and all that was theirs is ours." He tucked a carving knife he had been using into his belt and followed Brown Wing out the door.

As they reached the barn, Brown Wing gestured at the many chickens that were clawing and pecking at the dirt floor of the barn. "You get the horses hitched up and I will catch us a few chickens." He picked one up, rung its neck and threw it in the back of the wagon, its flopping wings flinging blood around on the board planks of the wagon bed.

When the wagon was loaded the prizes included guns, gun powder, a box of lead sheets for pouring musket balls, cooking pots and utensils, both metal and wood. Blankets were also a prize. They took dried meat and smoked meat from the smokehouse and storage cellar. They also loaded cornmeal, flour, dried apples and potatoes. They gathered the riding horses they found in the pasture and tied them to the back of the wagon.

Runs Against Something When Crawling stepped up into the driver's seat of the wagon and snapped the reins.

Breaks Up came out of the cabin and sprang up

into the seat next to Runs Against Something When Crawling and handed him a leather bound Bible.

The driver scoffed, "What are you doing? Are you becoming a cut-hair? Why do you bring this?"

Breaks Up opened the Bible and tore out a page. He spindled the page around a finger twisting closed the open end. He withdrew it from his finger and held it out so the driver could see. "This is very fine paper and will make very good powder measures for when the squaws are making bullets." He shook the Bible in the air. "And look how much paper is in this book."

Runs Against Something When Crawling shrugged his shoulders in agreement.

The little band was off, leaving their victims, stripped of clothing and dismembered, where they fell.

Brown Wing rode up next to the wagon and spoke to Breaks Up as Ghost Killer came up next to him leading Breaks Up's pony. "What do we do if we meet someone on the road?"

Ghost Killer heard the question and raised the rifle he had taken from Baker and shook it in the air with defiance. "We shall kill them!"

Breaks Up dropped the Bible he was holding next to Runs Against Something When Crawling and slipped from the seat onto his pony. "I will ride ahead. If we meet someone, we will pull off the road and hide if possible. If that's not possible, we will place ourselves and our ponies between the road and the wagon so it is not recognized."

Ghost Killer shrugged, made a growling noise and pulled his reins, falling behind the wagon.

It was late in the evening when they crossed Crow Creek and entered the village of Shakopee, their Chief.

Breaks Up was riding ahead of the others, so he went to the lodge of Chief Shakopee and told him of the deed that had been done. By the time the wagon got into the village, several fires burned brightly and children ran around in joy and anticipation of the prize food soon to fill their hungry stomachs.

With chickens on cooking fires, it was as if a great celebration had been declared. There was food for everyone as Ghost Killer told his story of the deed that had been done and excitement filled every lodge.

Chief Shakopee went into his lodge and stayed there for several minutes. When he came out he spoke to the people. "This is a matter to be discussed with a war chief. I am taking the young men to Chief Little Crow. You must tell him your story."

Several young men went with them the two miles from the Redwood Agency to the house of Little Crow.

Awakened in the middle of the night, Little Crow sat up in his bed and listened to all four versions of the story carried by the young men. After a moment of thought he stood.

"You have declared war. You did this by the blood

you shed. You have broken the treaty and the allotment payment for all of the people will be stopped. Because you have killed women, the white soldiers will come seeking a dreadful vengeance."

He pointed to the young men standing before him. "Go quickly and bring all the chiefs here for a council -- a council of war."

By three in the morning, the chiefs from all of the villages of the Santee Sioux Nation were gathered for the council. There were approximately one hundred and fifty chiefs representing the 7,000 tribal members that lived on and near the reservation.

After Ghost Killer told his story, Little Crow spoke.

"It is war. War must be declared by this council. We must kill all the whites and the cut-hairs who claim them as friends and refuse to fight against them."

Chief Shakopee rose and answered the raging Little Crow. "The Sissetons and the Wahpetons are opposed to fighting. Many of us are members of the Church and have had successful farms for many years. Chief Little Crow himself is a member of the Episcopal Church. He was a signer of the great treaty and he has been to meet with the white president, Buchanan. If you choose to make war on the cut-hairs, you will face the Sissetons and the Wahpetons before you face the white man. There are many purebloods as well as mixed-bloods against this war."

Chiefs Wabasha and Wacouta, like Shakopee,

spoke for peace, but they too, were quickly shouted down.

As the sun was rising, Little Crow stepped forward, a powerful leader in his own tribe, husband to twenty wives, father of twenty-six children and now, leader of his people. "War is declared. Those who have friends among the whites have my permission to warn them to leave our country. I have spoken for attacking the Army posts at Fort Ridgely and Sioux Falls first, but I have been out voted. There are more valuables to be taken by attacking settlers in the town of New Ulm. We will attack the Agency at Redwood Crossing in the morning."

A shout of adoration went up from the crowd gathered to hear the proceedings. War parties formed and dashed away in the darkness to kill settlers. The women began to make bullets and the men started cleaning their guns.

That morning, a large war party led by Chief Little Crow left for the Redwood Crossing Agency.

Chief Shakopee, Big Eagle and several members of his band came to the site to witness what was happening.

Chief Little Crow directed the onslaught against the Agency. He was very angry because Mr. Andrew Myrick, the trading post master with an Indian wife, had refused credit to some hungry Indians a short time before when they asked him for supplies. He said, "Go eat grass."

As Big Eagle watched, the trader exited the building, trying to escape through a small door in the roof.

The man had been seen by Chief Little Crow, who sent two braves from his side to kill the trader and stuff his mouth with grass.

Little Crow turned to the chief's watching and said, "Who is eating grass now? Are your warriors cowards? There is great plunder and supplies to be divided by the winners of this fight."

Anxious, but loyal braves looked questioningly at their chiefs. Both Shakopee and Big Eagle could see the doors had been breached and dead and mutilated bodies lay on the ground in front of the trading post. Their braves had not participated in the killing.

In unison, the chiefs lowered their heads, a sign of consent and their braves charged, letting out war whoops.

Big Eagle turned to Chief Shakopee, "Myrick is eating grass and we are now committed. We must go along and do the best we can."

Chief Shakopee stared at the jubilation and destruction in front of him and turned to Big Eagle. "I fear that we have made a grave error by starting this war. The whites will surely come and wipe the people out to the last man."

Big Eagle wheeled his horse, "We must tell the cut-hairs among us who will not fight and the warriors who have friends among the whites that they must get out of this country because this is war."

During the first day of killing the Dakotas massacred unsuspecting farm families, killing forty-four and taking ten captive to be used as slaves or traded later. Fort Ridgely and the town of New Ulm were also attacked. Panicking settlers fled eastward from twenty-three counties, leaving the southwestern Minnesota frontier virtually unpopulated except for the barricaded areas of Fort Ridgely and New Ulm. The garrison at Sioux Falls was wiped out to the last man.

On August 18th: over 400 unprepared and poorly armed civilians were killed on the frontier. At the Lower Agency the dead included a physician, women and children.

Having the uprising reported to Fort Ridgely on the 18th of August, Captain John Marsh rode into the field with forty-six mounted infantry troopers and an interpreter. His company rode into an ambush and was attacked at Redwood Ferry as they approached the lower Agency. Here, twenty-three members of the unit lost their lives including Marsh who drown in the Minnesota River.

During the day and night, settlements along the Minnesota and Cottonwood Rivers in Renville County and Beaver, Sacred Heart and LaCroix Creek were all raided. At mid-night the looting of Yellow Medicine took place.

Tuesday August 19th: John Other Day, a cut-hair leading whites, departed from Yellow Medicine at dawn. That day 4,000 settlers began flight from all parts of the area.

On Wednesday, August 20th: The first attack on New Ulm and Fort Ridgley took place. On this day, settlers from the Shetek Lake area were surrounded at "slaughter slough" and killed. Of this group, Mrs. Esleck survived.

On Thursday, August 21st: The attacks at Big Stone Lake, Eagle Lake, and other more distant localities took place. Hundreds of whites were slaughtered.

On Friday, August 22: Over 300 refugees poured into Fort Ridgley. The same day a major attack took place there. The Riggs party from counties to the north reached Fort Ridgley, but decided to continue down river.

On August 23: New Ulm was attacked a second time by the Dakota, but this time the residents were ready and drove the Indians off. This attack left most of the town burned to the ground, with two thousand refugees, mostly women and children. They, along with wounded men, set off in wagons and on foot for Mankato, thirty miles away.

Colonel Sibley, leading Minnesota volunteers, ignored the request from besieged New Ulm for aid, and proceeded to St. Peter to await reinforcements.

On August 26: Governor Alexander Ramsey ordered Colonel Henry Sibley, himself a former governor of the state, to take an army complement of Minnesota volunteers that had been scheduled to go south into the Civil War and capture or wipe out the Indians involved.

On August 27: Colonel Sibley advanced from the east with 1,500 soldiers toward Fort Ridgely.

On Thursday, August 28th: Colonel Sibley arrived at Fort Ridgley lifting the Dakota siege, and began the second phase of the Dakota Conflict-- an organized American military effort to defeat and punish the Sioux.

On September 2nd: Two companies of troops were surrounded in Birch Coulee and assailed in a dawn attack. Thirty-one hours later after the start of the attack on September 3rd, a relief party from Fort Ridgley reached Birch Coulee. In the coulee thirty-three people lay dead or mortally wounded.

On Sept. 9, 1862: Governor Ramsey, furious over the killing of roughly 677 settlers and 77 soldiers on the western frontier, said in an address to the state Legislature: "The Sioux Indians of Minnesota must be exterminated or driven forever beyond the borders of this state."

At this time the Legislature placed a bounty of $500 on the head of Little Crow, dead or alive.

Also on the 9th: Dakota massacres took place at Acton, Hutchinson, and Fort Abercrombie.

On Thursday, September 18: 1600 troops led by Colonel Sibley marched toward Yellow Medicine after getting munitions and supplies from Fort Ridgley.

On Thursday, September 18th: A debate occurred among the Indians whether to kill or surrender the captives, while the Indians that wanted to surrender sent messages to Sibley urging him to hurry.

On September 23rd: The Indians tried a morning ambush of Sibley's column and failed. About one third of Sibley's troops saw action.

By mid-September, the initiative had shifted to the Federal forces.

On September 23: In a decisive battle at Wood Lake,700 to 1,200 Dakota warriors were forced to withdraw after suffering heavy casualties.

Meanwhile, divisions among the Dakota on the war increased. To the north, chiefs of the Upper Agency Sisseton and Wahpeton continued to oppose the fighting. Chiefs Red Iron and Standing Buffalo threatened to fire upon any of Little Crow's followers that entered their area.

During the Wood Lake Battle, Dakotas friendly to the whites and opposed to the war were able to seize control of white captives and bring them back to their own camp. They released 269 white prisoners to the control of Colonel Sibley.

On September 24: Little Crow and hundreds of other participants of the outbreak departed for Canada, Devils Lake, or for the western plains.

Surrounded to the north and south, facing severe food shortages and declining morale, many Dakota warriors chose to surrender. Together with those taken captive, the ranks of Dakota prisoners soon swelled to nearly 1,400. The six-week war was over. These fourteen hundred braves believed to have taken part in the raids in southern Minnesota in the late summer, early fall of 1862 were imprisoned at Fort Mankato.

Whites survivors were brought back to identify and press charges against their attackers, which they knew. A five man military court was appointed by Colonel Sibley and over three hundred Indians were sentenced to hang.

President Lincoln had his clerks review every case and commuted the death sentences of all but thirty-nine who had been convicted of the worst crimes, rape, murder and particular brutality. In one such atrocity a nine months pregnant woman was stripped naked, tied to a rail fence, her stomach sliced open, her unborn child removed and impaled on a stake while the woman's four year old son watched.

Thirty-eight were hanged on December 26, 1862. This was the largest mass execution in US history.

In April, 1863, the rest of the Dakota were expelled from Minnesota to Nebraska and South Dakota. The United States Congress abolished their reservations.

Little Crow was not among the Dakotas put on trial for his part in the massacres of 1862. He, along with 150 of his followers, fled to present-day North Dakota and Canada.

In June 1863, Little Crow returned to Minnesota to steal horses. Undetected and unopposed he began a leisurely life back in Minnesota. On July 3, a farmer shot Little Crow while the Dakota Chief picked berries with his son near Hutchinson. The farmer received a $500 reward from the state of Minnesota.

# Red Cloud's War

Red Cloud was the Sioux war chief who absolutely refused to sign a treaty with the white man until he had removed the three forts, C. F. Smith, Phil Kearny and Reno from the Powder River Country.

The massacre of Fetterman's column took place under his direction and he was concerned that the whites would not leave the area until the forts along the Bozeman Trail had been destroyed. As spring and summer broke across Montana he ordered increased raids against the forts and the parties that were outside of the forts. His raiding parties made dashes feeling out the weak spots.

He waited for the gathering of the nations in the Powder River Country which took place in late July. After J.R. Porter arrived at Ft. Phil Kearny with the new Model 1866 Springfield Trapdoor single shot breech-loading rifles and 100,000 rounds of .50 caliber ammunition. These arms and ammunition were quickly distributed from Fort Casper to Fort C. F. Smith. Even though there was little or no practice of marksmanship by the army at the forts, the new rifles gave the men a renewed feeling of confidence.

During the last week of July, Red Cloud sat in council with chiefs of the Cheyenne and Arapaho nations. It was decided that both Fort C. F. Smith and Fort Phil Kearny should be destroyed simultaneously during the first week of August. Any troops found outside of the forts would be destroyed and then the forts themselves would be attacked and burned with none of the occupants left alive.

The force of the combined band would then move against Fort Reno. Red Cloud ordered a force of 600 Cheyenne and 200 Sioux braves under the leadership of a Cheyenne chief to attack C. F. Smith while he led a band of 1200 against Fort Phil Kearny.

On August 1, 1867, Lieutenant Sigismund Sternberg led a patrol of 19 troopers and 6 civilians out to the hay fields two and a half miles from Fort C. F. Smith for the purpose of harvesting the crop. The riding horses of the troops were placed into a 100 by 60 foot corral of poles and cross-thatched willows.

About 10 AM an alert cavalryman gave the alarm when a band of Indians was seen approaching at a high rate of speed on horseback. One witness reported, "It was obvious they didn't want to parley. They were wearing paint and screaming war cries at the top of their lungs." Lieutenant Sternberg ordered everyone into the corral and as the war party approached firing arrows at the men, he ordered "Fire!" and "Fire at will."

Fifteen or twenty braves fell from their horses with the first volley. There was no hesitation on the part of the remaining warriors. They continued the charge thinking that the soldiers were using the old fashioned muzzle loading rifles. If they were, the braves would reach the corral and be among the defenders before they could get off a second shot. To their shock and dismay, they had just resumed their charge when a second volley sent another dozen braves rolling in the hay.

The rapid firing breech-loading .50 caliber Springfield carbines surprised the Indians. They left their horses and tried several attacks on foot but were repulsed with severe losses. This failing, they lit the hay field on fire near the corral to engulf the troopers in the direct path of the flames, but the wind shifted and sent the fire in another direction.

The corral fence stood only as high as a man's lowest rib. Lieutenant Sternberg insisted on standing up to direct the actions of his troops. He was warned several times by Al Colvin, a Civil War veteran, to keep a low profile. He refused and ended up shot through the head. The next in command took over. Sergeant Navin, who followed the example of his superior, and was killed almost immediately. Colvin, an expert rifleman, equipped with a 16 shot lever action Henry rifle took charge when the sergeant fell. During the fight he fired over 300 rounds from his Henry.

He commanded that the men get down as close to the ground as possible allowing them to fire over the lowest rail of the corral. Many times the Indians withdrew to a safe distance behind a bluff and fired volleys of arrows that arched high and fell like "black rain" inside the corral. It was during one of these attacks that a civilian hay cutter, J. C. Hollister, and an army private were killed.

The battle raged on until late afternoon when the fort noticed the hay party was not back in time for dinner. A relief column, firing a mountain howitzer, sent the Indians scattering in retreat.

The losses during this battle were, from 21 soldiers and 6 civilians: 2 soldiers killed 1 civilian killed 4 wounded. Indian Casualties are estimated of Cheyenne & Sioux: 600- 800 Warriors: 30-50 killed, 300 wounded.

Indians always managed to carry off all of their dead and wounded so there never was an actual account of their losses.

The morning of July 31, Captain James Powell, commanding company C of the 26th Infantry with 51 infantrymen marched out of Fort Phil Kearny.

There had been little Indian activity in the area for the past month and the company was light hearted as they marched out on a 30 day assignment to watch over the civilian wood cutting contractors working at Piney Island, some five miles from Fort Phil Kearny.

The woodcutters had a corral of 14 wagon boxes that normally sat atop wagon carriages. The corral sat on flat ground, about a half mile from the actual wood cutting and gathering site on Piney Island where the civilians had their main camp. The corral made an oval 60 feet long and 25 feet wide.

The sides of the wagon boxes were 4 feet high with peep holes bored in the outboard sides. Kegs, bags of grain and other items fortified the outboard sides.

Captain Powell set up his headquarters at the corral, his men's tents arranged around it. He assigned a sergeant and a 12 man patrol to go to the woodcutters camp, another sergeant with 13 men to be on escort duty for the loaded wagons heading to the fort. First Lieutenant John C. Jenness and the remaining 26 men remained at the corral.

On the evening of August 1, 1867, Chief Red Cloud and 1200 warriors camped on Lodge Trail Ridge near the scene of the Fetterman fight overlooking Fort Phil Kearny. His plan was to send a decoy party under the leadership of his nephew, Crazy Horse, to draw the soldiers into a trap, much as had been done to the Fetterman column. Once in the open, a large body of warriors would close on the soldiers and wipe them out.

The plan failed when an impatient party of young braves attacked the woodcutters camp on Piney Island killing two soldiers. The remaining soldiers and wood cutters raised the alarm and bolted for the fort, bypassing the wagon box corral. The party that attacked the wood cutters camp took their prize of highly valued mules from the wood cutters and began to pillage the camp.

Two civilians from the fort had been out deer hunting, but seeing Indian smoke signals, they went straight to the wagon box corral. There were now twenty-eight soldiers, two fleeing wood cutters and the two deer hunters inside the corral - a total of 32 men.

Sixty braves on horseback attacked the corral, throwing lassoes on tent poles as they rode through, flattening the army encampment. A second wave of attackers rode directly down onto the corral firing dozens of arrows and heaving lances.

The men inside the makeshift fort soon organized and began to fire at the onslaught, Captain Powell at one end of the corral and Lieutenant Jenness at the other.

Two or three dozen warriors were quickly knocked from their ponies by the rapid fire of the .50 caliber carbines. After two or three charges on horseback, the field now littered with dead and dying men and horses, the Indians withdrew to the safety of a nearby ravine. Pine pitch tipped arrows were lit and fired into the corral igniting hay and mule dung causing an almost unbearable stench.

Leaving their horses and stripping to the waist, some taking off all their clothing, the Indians came over the ridge attacking in a 'V' formation. They let out blood curdling war cries and charged the soldiers as fast as they could. The withering fire of the soldiers using the new Springfield rifles raked the formation causing it to fall apart and withdraw when it was within five feet of the fortification.

Laying concealed at the edge of the ravine that dropped off into Piney Valley, several Indian marksmen used muzzle loaders taken from the Fetterman fight. It was these marksmen that accounted for the deaths of Lieutenant Jenness and Privates Henry, Haggerty and wood cutter Thomas Boyle, all shot in the head.

Meanwhile, at Fort Phil Kearny, the lookouts up on Pilot Hill had observed the fight and alerted the fort. Near noon, Major Benjamin Smith and 103 soldiers came out of the fort to reinforce the soldiers in the wagon boxes. Smith brought 10 wagons driven by armed civilians and a mountain howitzer. It was presumed by the fort's commander that all the men at the wagon box corral would be dead. Major Smith approached, firing the mountain howitzer at the Indians he could see as he neared the corral.

The hostiles withdrew and Smith advanced without opposition to the corral, collecting the men there, and returning to Fort Phil Kearny. Additional civilian survivors, who had hidden in the woods during the battle, made it back to the fort after dark. Rescuers reported that the faces of the men from the fight were covered in black ash soot from the back flash of their guns.

The fight lasted four and a half hours and ended with the death of 7 whites and 2 wounded. The official records say Indian loses were 60 dead, 120 wounded.

Red Cloud said he lost the cream of his army that day. In later years, interviews with Indians indicated that there may have been as many as 1000 casualties at the wagon box fight. This was the last fight of Red Cloud's War.

In 1868 President Grant ordered Fort Phil Kearny, Fort C F Smith and Fort Reno be closed and abandoned. A band of Cheyenne warriors burned Fort Phil Kearny.

Through the Laramie treaty of 1868 all the land that had been taken from the Sioux, Cheyenne and Arapaho in the Powder River Country was returned to the Indians with no concessions to the US Government. Red Cloud had won his war.

# About The Authors

**Meredith I. Anderson,** author, historian and licensed Chef's Aid, was born in Osceola, Missouri. A graduate of Weber State University in Ogden, Utah, he was the president of the state wide organization, League of Utah Writers in 2007. His book, **MORE THAN A JOB, AN ADVENTURE** won the coveted Gold Quill for Literature Award. This book is available on Amazon.com, createspace.com, Barnes & Noble and Kindle. This book is also an audio book available from Audible.com and itunes. A Vietnam veteran, Meredith left active duty with the Navy as a Storekeeper Second Class (E5). He has spent the last forty years as a journalist, writing magazine and newspaper columns about fishing, hunting, camping and cooking to entertain the outdoor enthusiast. He makes his home with his wife of over 50 years in Osceola, MO.

**Linda Pool Anderson,** novelist and historian, has released her newest Trilogy, **They Were Lawmen: The Outlaw Trail** is the first book. A graduate of the University of Utah, she is a retired commercial airline pilot and Director of Flight Operations for the third largest regional freight airline in the US. They flew mail and UPS throughout the Rocky Mountain West and Hawaii.

THEY WERE
LAWMEN: THE
OUTLAW TRAIL

LINDA POOL ANDERSON

The true Story of two brothers, Charles and Abel Barnhill, who rode out of Fort Smith, Arkansas into the badlands of Indian Territory in pursuit of outlaws, murderers, thieves and bootleggers for the court of Judge Isaac Parker, the hanging judge.

Written from court records, newspapers and journals from the time, this book was three years in research and two years in writing and publication. *A Great Read...*

# Some books by these authors:

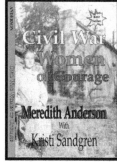

More Than A Job, An Adventure

Meredith "Ike" Anderson

**Not a war** story, but the story of a young man's adventures during a time of war. Follow Pete from a catastrophic mining disaster in Utah to the rolling deck of an American "Man of War."

He told his mining boss, "I'm going to get a job where they won't have to dig me up to bury me." And so, the story begins and becomes a page turning adventure that you can enjoy.

**After the Civil War**, the Indian Territory became a sanctuary for villains seeking refuge from the laws of their native state. At the time, the law of the land was written in such a manner as to prevent non-Indian outlaws from being arrested or prosecuted by Indian courts. As a result, the Indian Territory was the perfect place for ruthless men escaping justice to hide.

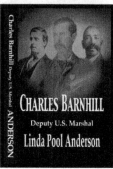

CHARLES BARNHILL
Deputy U.S. Marshal
Linda Pool Anderson

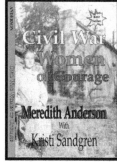

A collection of thirteen short stories about young women, ages 11 to 24. Each story is from newspaper clippings, reports and letters written during America's greatest conflict. Yes, the true events have been fictionalized somewhat to give the characters personality and voice. This book is designed especially for readers, grade 8 and above. This version of this book is currently being used by a local university as recommended reading in their History Department.

The American Civil War, one of the most violent wars ever contested, started in reality in 1850, when the Compromise of 1850 deposed the Missouri Compromise of 1820 and made **"Popular Vote,"** the way by which the decision would be made, to designate a state FREE or SLAVE.

Bushwhackers of Missouri

General Order 11

MEREDITH ANDERSON

Kansas became the test, northerners and southerner both pouring into the territory, voting to make that new state what either side preferred. Soon, bands of armed men rode through Kansas and Missouri, most from the anti-slavery north, the 'Red Legs' and 'Jayhawkers.' Other bands, representing the pro-slavery point of view, rode in from Missouri. These "border ruffians," soon known as 'bushwhackers,' like the 'Red Legs,' killed and burned out people with an opposite point of view.

**The stories** written in this book are typical of those found throughout history. The explorers of the Old World discovered a continent that was new to them and they jabbed their flag into the ground and claimed that land for their sovereign. There was no regard for the native peoples of that land.

At first, welcoming the Spanish, Dutch, Portuguese, French and English onto their shores, the Indians soon discovered that the strangers in their land were not there to live peacefully beside the Indian. The newcomers' interests lay in taking the riches of The New World back to their home country, controlling the land and dominating and subduing the native people.

When war broke out between two white factions, many times the Indians chose the losing side because they were promised the return of their lands if they won. When the wars were over, the white losers were banished back to where they came from while the Indian was more feared and hated than ever before.

**The story of twelve year-old** Annie Jewel Bounds, taken from letters and publications of the time. Annie would have gone off to war with her father, but when he was lost in battle, she convinces her mother to allow her to dress as a Yankee drummer boy and march off with a unit that is scheduled for discharge in just six weeks.

Her adventure places her in the thick of the fire and smoke at the Battle of Wilson's Creek, a few miles from Springfield, Missouri. Fought on August 10, 1861, it is the first 'real' battle of the Civil War., sometimes labelled the 'Bull Run' of the west. The 'Battle of Oak Hill,' as it was called by the Confederates, was a victory for the south. The better armed, trained and equipped Union Army lost a quarter of their forces against a foe twice their size.

**Hearing the hoofbeats** of twenty horses entering the yard at the front of her house, Mattea pulled the lead rope, releasing the cow she was milking and ran into the house to find five Sioux braves wearing war paint sitting at her table, smoking her husband's tobacco from the humidor on the mantle.

Mattea repressed her anger and shock. "Cinder Horse, why have you come to my home? And coming in without being invited." "Remember," he said in a stern voice, "do not go near the lodges of the settlement! Do not go near the Post Road and do not give an alarm or you and your children will die." He prodded her with the tip of his war lance. "Go! Go to your mother!"

**You can order** an autographed copy of any of the books written by Meredith and Linda Anderson and you won't have to pay the list price.

Simply mark the order form on the next page and send check or money order to the authors at:

Make checks payable to:

# L & M Anderson
# 825 Outer Lyons Private Road
# Osceola, MO 64776

**Phone: 417-664-0012**
Email: Linda
linda.skymama@gmail.com
Andy
fisherman.anderson@juno.com

Many of our books are also available as **Audiobooks.** **They** are available from **Audible.com, Amazon.com,** and **itunes.**

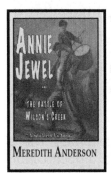   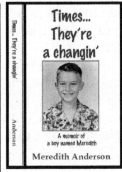

You can order any of these books at a special price by filling out the order form on the opposite page. ☞

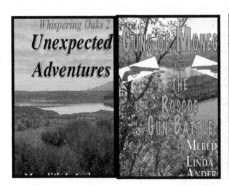  

# Order Form

| Titles by Meredith Anderson | RETAIL | Price | order QTY |
|---|---|---|---|
| Annie Jewel and The Battle. of Wilson's Creek | 16.99 | 10.00 | |
| **Bushwhackers of Missouri. and General Order 11** | 16.99 | 10.00 | |
| Fire Hair. | 16.99 | 10.00 | |
| **General Order Eleven, 1863 .** | 16.99 | 10.00 | |
| Ozarkia Cooking... | 16.99 | 10.00 | |
| Ozarkia Cooking 2... | 18.99 | 1200 | |
| Times... They're a changin'.... | 16.99 | 10.00 | |
| **Uprising** | 16.99 | 10.00 | |
| **University** Edition, Civil War Women of Courage | 16.99 | 10.00 | |
| Guns of Monegaw and the Roscoe Gun Battle | 16.99 | 10.00 | |
| Cherokee... | 16.99 | 10.00 | |
| Vietnam Edition, More Than. a Job, An Adventure | 16.99 | 10.00 | |
| **Whispering Oaks 2, Unexpec**ted Adventures | 16.99 | 10.00 | |
| Whispering Oaks, The Curse.. | 16.99 | 10.00 | |
| More Than a Job, An Adventure | 21.99 | 15.00 | |
| **Author: Linda Anderson** | | | |
| **They were Lawmen: The outlaw trail...** | 16.99 | **10.00** | |
| **Brothers of the Badge** | 16.99 | 10.00 | |
| Killers on the loose | 1699 | 10.00 | |
| **Charles Barnhill, Deputy US** Marshal | 24.99 | 20.00 | |

Order $_____

Please add **$3** for the first book and **$2** for each
additional book for Shipping & Handling ................... $_____

Note to Author: Sign dedication to:   **Total Order $_____**

_____

 Cut along dotted line.

**L & M Anderson**
**825 Outer Lyons Private Road**
**Osceola, MO 64776**